WORSHIP-CENTERED TEACHING

GUIDING YOUTH TO DISCOVER THEIR IDENTITY IN CHRIST

JIM HAMPTON
AND
RICK EDWARDS
EDITORS

Beacon Hill Press of Kansas City
and

WordAction Publishing Company™
Kansas City, Missouri

Copyright 2001
by Beacon Hill Press of Kansas City

ISBN 083-411-9013

Printed in the United States of America

Cover design: Paul Franitza

Library of Congress Cataloging-in-Publication Data

Worship-centered teaching : guiding youth to discover their identity in Christ / Jim Hampton and Rick Edwards, editors.
    p. cm.
  Includes bibliographical references.
  ISBN 0-8341-1901-3 (pb.)
    1. Church work with youth. 2. Youth—Religious life. I. Hampton, Jim, 1966- II. Edwards, Rick, 1954-
  BV4447 .W69 2001
  268'.433—dc21

          2001035439

10   9   8   7   6   5   4   3   2   1

This book is dedicated to the many guides who have walked, and continue to walk, alongside us. Thanks for modeling what it means to be Christian and helping us follow God's plan for our lives. It is because of your investment in us that this book is possible.

What I most appreciate about this book is the way it brings together the three key components essential for effective youth ministry training: a thoughtful appraisal of current youth culture, a response to that culture shaped by biblical/theological thinking, and an integration of these insights with everyday, "real world" youth ministry. Youth workers both paid and volunteer will find in these pages a mind-set and a strategy for making worship more than just the standard "half-hour of standing while we sing slow songs with our eyes closed." In a culture where worship often becomes more self-focused than God-focused—just a step above "Curious George Visits the Holy Land"—this resource reminds us that the Bible is God's Story, the focus is God's glory, and the invitation is to become a part of this great Story. If you're looking to help your students get a bigger picture of the biggest story, you will find this material helpful. Enjoy the adventure.

Duffy Robbins, associate professor of youth ministry, Eastern College

These are days of opportunity for youth ministry. The millennial generation is craving significant relationships. *Worship-Centered Teaching* is about helping youth make those connections with the most important influences in their lives (i.e., the family, significant adult mentors, the faith community, the biblical story, and the Holy Spirit). This book is more than a practical approach to teaching. It lays a comprehensive foundation for *being* a good teacher as well as *acting* like one. *Worship-Centered Teaching* is good theology, good Christian education, and good youth ministry.

Ed Robinson, dean of the faculty and professor of Christian education,
Nazarene Theological Seminary

An engaging and formative approach to Christian education that reclaims the Church's calendar of worship as a clue to experiencing the great Christian Story. A powerful means of God's grace!

Thomas H. Groome, professor of theology and religious education, Boston College

I am thrilled to have a teaching tool that is built on the foundation of *guiding* students in their encounter with Christ. *Worship-Centered Teaching* recognizes that discovering one's identity in Christ is a process of shepherding students into the presence of God.

Helen Musick, author, speaker, and instructor in youth ministry, Asbury Seminary

Contents

Introduction

R I C K   E D W A R D S

A few days before Christmas 2000, Justin Johnson, a 16-year-old student from Overland Park, Kansas, left the comfort and holiday cheer of his suburban home and traveled for 26 hours by air to an airport near Arusha, Tanzania. His ultimate destination was the glacier-covered summit of Mount Kilimanjaro, at 19,340 feet above sea level, the highest point on the continent of Africa (*Kansas City Star* 2000).

From Arusha, Justin took a Land Rover, dodging potholes in the 50-mile dirt road to the base of Kilimanjaro. To reach the summit, Justin walked, hiked, and climbed 30 more miles through five climate zones, ranging from plains (80 to 90 degrees F.), through tropical rain forests, to arctic conditions at the summit (0 to 35 degrees without windchill). He carried 50 pounds of boots, goggles, books, camera equipment, sets of clothing for every climate change, plus an extensive medical kit. (In addition to almost certain altitude sickness, Justin faced the threats of mosquito-borne illnesses such as malaria and yellow fever; viral infections such as polio and measles; and hepatitis A or typhoid, from contaminated food or water.)

As exciting and adventurous as this journey sounds, it is also obvious that Justin faced considerable difficulties and some bona fide, life-threatening dangers. Not many teenagers would be up to such a challenge. Yet, there is one journey that all teenagers undertake that is filled with its own adventures and dangers. We call it adolescence. The stages and changes that teenagers go through are just as dramatic and shocking to one's system as climate changes on Kilimanjaro. The threats to their physical health range from injury and disease to violence, abuse, and neglect. Psychological and emotional problems plague them as much as any tropical disease does travelers in Africa. Spiritually, the journey through adolescence can bring a person to not only breathtaking views of God in mountaintop experiences but also the opportunity to fall from grace. Both extremes have significant, lifelong effects.

Wisely, Justin had companions for his journey. He trained and traveled with his dad, Jeff. In Africa, they hired 10 porters to help carry their tents, food, and other equipment. In addition to the porters, the Johnsons hired two professional guides. These key people had made the trip several times before and knew the best routes to the summit. They knew the best places to camp, where to get water, and what to do in all sorts of situations brought about by rapid and dramatic changes in altitude, climate, and weather.

Guides who walk alongside teenagers are just as important during the years of adolescence as on a two-week trip to Africa. Sunday School teachers, Bible study and small-group leaders, youth pastors, youth sponsors, pastors, and other adults can be those guides. If you fit any of these descriptions, you have a vital role to play in the lives of the teenagers you know and serve. You have the experience, knowledge, and skills they need to make the journey from childhood through adolescence to adulthood.

This book aims to help you become a better guide; you might say it is a guide for guides. It will help any adult who works with teenagers, for it promotes a philosophy—or better yet, a *theology*—of ministry that provides a sound foundation for all phases of youth work. However, the specific focus of this book is on the ministry of teaching, the central core of any church's youth ministry. It will help youth workers (guides) who teach in any capacity, from Sunday School teachers who teach structured lessons every week, to youth pastors who lead midweek youth meetings, to volunteers who only occasionally teach.

Good teachers know their students, so the first chapter provides an overview of this generation. The next chapter provides a theological foundation for youth ministry, including teaching. The third chapter explores the issue of faith development during adolescence. The remaining chapters focus on topics that become more and more specific to the art and task of teaching, such as the proper role of the teacher, lesson planning, learning styles, and teaching methods.

We trust that you have a dedication to the ministry of teaching young people. We pray that this book will in some small way help you become a better guide for the students with whom you are traveling now. Of even greater help than any book is Jesus himself, who has gone ahead of us, blazing the trail for us to follow, and who promises mercy and grace to help us (Heb. 4:14-16). Lead on in confidence!

CHAPTER 1

WHO

ARE THE

MILLENNIALS?

A QUICK LOOK AT

THE STUDENTS YOU

ARE TEACHING

JIM HAMPTON

Introduction

In case you haven't noticed, there is an invasion going on—an invasion of teenagers. The number of teens in the United States aged 12 to 19 has increased each year since 1992 and is expected to hit 35 million by 2010 (Foster 1999). Not since the huge baby boom of the 1950s and 1960s has there been such an influx of young people. The general consensus is that this current growth began with students born after about 1980.[1] Not everyone agrees on when the number of births started to drop off, but several experts suggest closing the generation with children born in 1995. All told, this generation of young people numbers about 75 to 80 million in the United States alone.

In an effort to quantify this generation, various names have been assigned to it. Some have named this generation of students as generation Y (which naturally follows generation X, the preceding generation). Others have called this generation the baby boomlet or echo boomers, since most of these students' parents are baby boomers. The net generation is yet another popular name, primarily because these students are so Internet savvy. For this book we have chosen to describe this generation with the term *millennials*. We feel it is a term that signifies both hope and new beginnings, a perfect description for this generation.

Their Impact

Because of their numbers, millennials are putting a severe strain on school districts. Many school districts are using temporary buildings to accommodate all the students. Other districts have doubled or even tripled class sizes because of a lack of rooms and teachers. Many school districts are seeking levy increases to ensure they have adequate funding to handle the numbers of students coming through the ranks.

Millennials also have quite an impact on the economy. They spent $141 billion in 1998, which is up 16 percent over 1997 (Associated Press 1999). Of that amount, teenagers actually earned about $121 billion; the other $20 billion dollars came mostly from their parents. In addition, millennials influence the spending of even larger amounts of money, primarily through their parents and siblings. Overall, millennials spend or influence the spending of $500 billion annually.

Millennials and Previous Generations

Millennials share some characteristics with the generation that preceded them, generation X. Both generations are heavily into music, movies, and television.[2] And while the students of generation X were certainly computer savvy, the millennials are redefining what it means to be computer literate.[3] This generation will be the first to feel more at home in front of the computer than in front of the television.

While there are some similarities between millennials and the Xers, this generation also shares some of the same tastes and interests as their boomer parents. Retro fashions are everywhere. (Don't you wish you'd saved those bell-bottoms?) Mainstream advertising uses images and music that were popular in the 1960s and 1970s. Pop groups are recording hit remakes of music from that era. Some television shows are featuring "turn back the clock" or "retro" episodes, while others go all the way and create shows about that time period. Millennials eat this stuff up.

> Millennials are not yet who they are going to be.

In some ways, millennials are even more conservative than their parents. They are less apt to participate in abusive lifestyles such as drug or alcohol abuse, or to engage in sexual promiscuity before marriage. They do not hold the same type of antiestablishment sentiments that their boomer parents held, but instead see the government and other institutions as agents of potential change.

Values/Characteristics

Now that we have reviewed a general description of millennials, let's examine some of the specific values and characteristics that are unique to them. One caution is in order, however. It is still too early in the process to accurately predict who they will become. Some experts believe strongly that this generation will be the next hero generation, much like the World War II generation. Others believe that this generation will turn out to be just like the Xers who preceded them, only with better defense mechanisms. Simply put, millennials are not yet who they are going to be.

Because we don't know for certain how this generation of teenagers will turn out, we will first describe each unique characteristic of this generation and then show how that characteristic might work itself out, both positively and negatively. This will give us a good understanding of this generation, no matter who they eventually become.

Diversity

The U.S. population is increasingly multicultural.[4] The number of African-Americans in the United States is fairly stable. Latino and Asian populations are rapidly increasing in size and influence.[5] These multicultural populations will be concentrated in select areas. African-Americans will be prevalent in the urban cores and in the old deep south states. Latinos will continue to increase in the southwestern border states (e.g., California, Arizona, New Mexico, Texas), as well as in Florida and in western areas where migrant agricultural workers are needed. Asian populations will be most visible in West Coast states and eastern coastal cities.

If you don't live in one of those areas, you may not notice these population changes much. Despite their geographic concentration, however, these cultural groups will have an influence far beyond their geographic location. For instance, salsa has recently overtaken ketchup as the number 1 condiment, and tacos are now as popular as hamburgers. Clothing lines such as Fubu and Esco are worn by teenagers of all groups. Music styles ranging from gangster rap to reggae are finding their way into the mainstream. Celebrities like Tiger Woods, Will Smith, Jennifer Lopez, and Lucy Liu have strong crossover appeal. While these changes may seem new to many of us, millennials accept them without a second thought and most students have friends who are not of their own ethnic or racial background.[6]

Advantages of Diversity

If we are willing to listen, millennials can teach the church how to get along with other cultural groups, creating more global Christians. In addition, millennials can help us learn things from other cultures that will enrich our own culture and faith. The Latino value of the family can enrich the church. African-American Christians model a faith that affects all aspects of life. Asian culture stresses discipline and perseverance, which are biblical values everyone can benefit from. As we learn from one another, our lives are strengthened, and we become better Christians.

Dangers of Diversity

Diversity can have some drawbacks. Millennials' willingness to accept others uncritically may cloud their ability to see non-Christian elements, such as those related to personal morality or important doctrines, in different cultures.

A possible negative response to diversity would be the rise of splinter or hate groups that are fueled by "fear of others." Such groups are moving more into the mainstream, drawing many teens into their webs of hate. Diversity may also result in more intercultural dating and marriage relationships, which may strain the understanding of older adults and the members of hate groups.

Tolerance

Millennials are open and accepting not only of other people but also of other ideas. They believe that every person has a right to his or her own ideas, beliefs, and behavior, and that one person's opinion, views, beliefs, or behavior is just as legitimate as another person's.

Advantages of Tolerance

Unconditional acceptance is one of God's virtues. Millennials can model this for us. Their acceptance and openness make communication with and understanding of others possible. In addition, this type of tolerance makes it easy to welcome non-Christians to church activities, where they are accepted without judgment.

Dangers of Tolerance

Millennials may be prone to swallowing ideas or following behaviors without thinking about whether they are consistent with Christian faith. Many of them think that tolerance means they must endorse or consent to different beliefs, or that they cannot disagree or critique those ideas or behaviors. However, we must help them understand that tolerance of other ideas is not the same as agreeing with them. Although God accepts people as they are, He will not allow them to stay the same.

Optimism

Millennials feel good about themselves, the future, and what they can do to shape the future. This is due to two factors: first, their parents have raised them with strong self-esteem (by doing things such as awarding trophies and medals just for participating in sports and activities). Second, for the most part, millennials have not known adversity. Organizations such as Mothers Against Drunk Driving (MADD), new child safety legislation, and awareness campaigns that ask, "Is It Good for the Children?" all seek to protect children and teens. Millennials have been raised in a good economy with low unemployment and have not faced a major war, such as World War II or Vietnam.

While millennials are optimistic, they are realistic at the same time. They believe they can make a difference in the world and want to do so, but they prefer to act locally in politics and community service.

Although the vast majority of millennials are happy and optimistic, there are some notable exceptions. These young people feel hopeless or depressed, have eating disorders, or may commit suicide or other acts of violence (e.g., the shootings in Columbine and Paducah).

Advantages of Optimism

Millennials may become the next hero generation (the last one was the World War II generation) who become actively involved in solving society's ills. They have the motivation and self-confidence to make a positive difference in the world. One class of elementary students who studied the issue of modern slavery decided to do something about the problem. Through a series of bake sales, walkathons, and other fund-raisers, they raised enough money to purchase the redemption of Sudanese slaves.

Desiring to make a difference, millennials respond well to opportunities to serve in service projects and mission trips. Youth workers would do well to provide such ministry opportunities for students.

Dangers of Optimism

Because they haven't experienced any major crises, millennial students may not have the skills or knowledge to react decisively when crises hit. When they face a problem or get in trouble, they may look to their elders to bail them out.

Collaboration

Millennials want to belong, and they like to work together as a team. Many have been educated in schools that use a cooperative learning curriculum, and most have participated on sports teams sometime in their childhood.

Family is important for this generation of students. Unlike generation Xers, millennial students like spending time with their parents. Furthermore, they trust their parents' judgment and really want to know what they think. Because of their need for belonging and acceptance, millennials will use positive peer pressure to solve problems. For example, colleges are now using a method called "social norming" to reduce drinking among students. When students are informed that their peers actually drink less than they assume, they reduce their own drinking behaviors. Drinking less, not more, becomes the cool thing to do. This positive peer pressure approach is being applied by other universities and by the U.S. Department of Education (Clayton 1997 and Franey 2000).

Advantages of Collaboration

Because of their need and desire for belonging and teamwork, millennials have a built-in preference for community, which is one of the primary values of the Christian faith. If they continue this collaboration, they will be able to work together to achieve larger goals than they could ever accomplish individually. Students are open to crossing denominational boundaries to work with fellow believers to reach a lost world with the gospel.

Dangers of Collaboration

Related to this issue, millennials may not appreciate denominational identity and loyalty as much as older generations do. Church leaders may find it more difficult to get millennials to commit across the board to denominational programs and procedures.

Although adolescents have always begun to separate from family and identify with their peers, millennials may be at risk of going too far in this direction. By exclusively identifying with and spending time with peers, today's students could potentially become a "tribe apart"[7] with no adult voices to guide and teach them how to be adults. Youth workers will need to encourage and equip parents to be the primary Christian educators/influencers of their teens.

Spirituality

Millennials believe there are other ways of knowing besides just reason. They give equal weight to other knowledge forms, such as intuition and emotions. Although this scares those who hold an Enlightenment view that science is the ultimate authority, the reality is that millennial students are very interested in the spiritual aspects of life. They want to have a personal encounter with the supernatural and are not content just to practice religion or focus mainly on doctrine and dogma.

As our world revolves increasingly around technology and electronic communication, these students will long for intimate relationships, both human and divine. Recent studies have repeatedly shown that the majority of young people say religion is important in their lives.

> Millennials approach worship expectantly, believing that God will show up.

Advantages of Spirituality

Students with this interest in spiritual matters will be open to talking about God and the claims of the gospel. However, please note that these students are not an "easy sell," content to just listen to an explanation of the gospel and then commit their lives to it. Instead, they want a thoughtful explanation, and they want to hear how God is working in your life.

A second advantage is that Christian students can teach the Church much about meaningful corporate worship. Because of their desire for personal encounters with the supernatural, they approach worship expectantly, believing that God will show up.

Dangers of Spirituality

An interest in spirituality does not automatically mean that one will become religious or involved in organized religion. For example, the percentage of teens attending weekly religious services dropped from 55 percent in 1986 to 42 percent in 1997 (Cimino and Lattin 1999).

Perhaps the greatest danger is that spirituality plus tolerance can result in a mix-and-match theology. Students may investigate various religions, pick the parts they like, and then form a personal faith composed of beliefs that beneath the surface contradict each other. Unfortunately, most students do not think deeply enough to see the contradictions that are readily apparent to adults.

Information Technology

In traditional cultures, adults kept certain knowledge from children until they were deemed ready to handle them. This included discussions of sex, dealing with the harsh reality of the world, as well as certain stories and traditions deemed appropriate only for adults. Now, students have access to, or are exposed to, much information that once was considered inappropriate for their age.

In terms of sheer amount, they are exposed to more information in a single day than medieval peasants were exposed to in their entire lifetime (Foster 1999). Most of this information comes from the media, the Internet, and their peer groups. Because of the ready accessibility these avenues offer, students can learn about anything their curiosity demands.

Advantages of Information Technology

It is much easier to communicate and exchange ideas with others worldwide. Technology tends to give women and those who are physically weaker more power. New technology has recently allowed those who are blind or deaf to utilize the Internet and computers.

The economic outlook is excellent for those who know how to use information technology. Furthermore, the rapid, easy communication that is available may make it easier to share the gospel in ways and places that were impossible before.

Dangers of Information Technology

As we are all too aware, a flood of data hardly equals wisdom. Because the information is unfiltered, students have a difficult time discerning the true and good from the vulgar and evil. Furthermore, they have little time for thoughtful reflection or conversation with adults to help them think through these issues. We need to teach our students how to control the influx of information and how to act on that which is beneficial.

The non college-educated may find it difficult to prosper in an information-based economy (except for those self-taught computer experts who own their own Internet businesses). Another potential problem is that overreliance on technology may leave millennials unable to cope when computers or cell phones break down.

Traditional Outlook

Millennials are "neotraditionalists," a new generation with old-fashioned concerns: friends, romance, money, and, above all, family. As a result, adolescent at-risk behavior is decreasing. Consider the following examples:

- Teen smoking and drug use have stabilized or dropped in the last few years.
- Teen pregnancy rate has dropped 17 percent since 1990.
- Teen abortion rate is down 31 percent since 1986.
- Violent crime committed by teens has dropped steadily since 1993 (Foster 1999).

In addition, millennials get along better with their parents than their parents or generation Xers did. A Clinique Labs survey of teen girls and their mothers showed similar responses on everything from values to career choices, with 90 percent reporting being "very happy with the relationship" they have with each other (Large 1999).

Advantages of a Traditional Outlook

Less risky behavior leads to healthier students, and better relationships with parents means fewer family crises. This means youth workers are able to focus more on spiritual formation and less on counseling, managing substance abuse, and other crises. And because families get along better, parents and teens can spend time bonding and learning from one another rather than fighting.

Dangers of a Traditional Outlook

Students may be too compliant, too conformist, and too complacent. As a result, some of them may be less ready to embrace a radical faith and act on it.

These descriptions are generalizations and may not describe all the students you work with. However, this can be a useful guide for understanding the students to whom we are ministering. Next, let's take a look at some ministry strategies that can enable us to best reach them.

Three Strategies for Reaching Millennial Students

Strategy 1—Take a Missional Approach to Ministry

Youth ministry in North America has long operated under a "Field of Dreams" model ("If you build it, they will come"). In the 1980s and 1990s, we built big youth centers and gyms, held laser tag nights, or sponsored big concerts in hopes that students would come and participate. We now recognize that most students will not seek out the church or be eager to participate just because it has great programs. Students will not be "wooed" into a lasting faith because we have great game nights or basketball leagues.

Instead, the church needs to seek teens, meet them where they are, invite them into a relationship with Jesus, and draw them into church life. To do this well, we must adopt a missionary mind-set. Like a missionary we must understand youth culture in order to assess its impact on students. For instance, when our students become involved in the latest cultural trends, we must readily identify the risks and harm they might face.

When we understand the culture, we can help students critically evaluate it and its message. Good youth workers will take the time to sit down with them and discuss the messages (both implicit and explicit) that are present in the movies, music, and television they are listening to and viewing.

When we understand the culture, we can also use what our students are familiar with to communicate the truths they need to hear. We can use clips from videos, pop music, or current events to open the discussion of a topic from a Christian perspective. This not only provides a common starting point (both students and teacher are familiar with the clip, song, or event) but can also reinforce the point we want to make. An added benefit is that when it is used in conjunction with discussion or other activity, several learning styles are used, which ensures that more students are catching the message. Chapter 6 gives more information on learning styles.

Strategy 2—Practice Incarnational Ministry

As our students move through adolescence to adulthood, they will need solid, familiar relationships with other adults. They especially need adults who see potential in them that they do not see themselves. Through the eyes of these adults, students can begin to discover who they really are.

Of course, no matter how good our relationship with our students may be, we can never take the place of their relationship with Christ. We must remember that our relationship with students is modeled on the fact that their relationship with God is the ultimate relationship. Both teacher and students can learn something about God through the context of our relationships with each other.

How do we begin to build this type of relationship with our students? First, we have to like our students, not just love them. To love our students is simply Christian, but to like them is the basis for a trustworthy relationship. This doesn't mean that we have to like everything they do or say, or that we have to like their music or clothing styles. It does mean that we must like them, genuinely like them, for who they are.

Second, we need to find common ground, a starting point that can bring us together and give us something to talk about. You and your student might both be into restoring cars or knitting or working at a Habitat for Humanity site; the list is endless. Find some areas where you have common interests and begin to build on that.

Third, commit to building long-term relationships. Too many youth workers initiate a relationship with a student, but when their life becomes busy, the relationship with the student is one of the first things dropped. Students need to know that the trusted adults in their lives (like you) will be there to help them through the rough terrain of life.

Our students desperately need a community of faith that encourages, challenges, and walks with them. Therefore, the fourth way we help foster incarnational relationships with our students is by providing opportunities for them to be together with the community of faith. But it is not enough just to gather; we must intentionally provide a caring, supporting environment at all times.

One place this can happen is in small groups. Most students are somewhat intimidated by large groups of people, and therefore will not be very open. However, when placed in a small group of people who openly care about them, most students will blossom. Here they learn what it means to care for others and to be cared for; how to support and be supported; and how to hold others and be held accountable for their spiritual health.

Another element of community is the congregation. We must be careful not to segregate our students from the life of the congregation. If we do everything as a separate youth group, our students will grow up knowing only adults who serve as youth sponsors. Then, when students graduate from the youth group they are thrust into a world of adults they don't know. As a result, they typically leave the church.

Instead, we must purposely seek to integrate students into the larger Christian body, allowing them not only to be involved in the services and activities of the whole church but also to build relationships with people of all ages.

Lastly, we have to trust God for the results. We can follow all the steps listed here, give tirelessly to the effort of building relationships, have students over at our house constantly, but still not see any change in their lives. In those instances, we must remember that we are not responsible for the results of our efforts. We are only responsible for making a good-faith effort. In the end, we simply have to trust that God will one day bring to fruition the seed of the gospel that we have planted and watered. Chapter 3 will discuss more specifically our role in this process.

Strategy 3—Build Your Life and Ministry Around the Story of God

Millennial students want a faith that can withstand life. As a result, pat answers are simply not acceptable to millennials. They don't want any part of the "Five Steps to Living the Christian Life." They know that life is complicated and messy and that a five-step approach isn't realistic. If youth do not see faith as relevant, they will shrug off any claims of the church with a disinterested "whatever."

These students learn well through stories, especially true stories. While storytelling should not be the only method we use, it can be an asset to any teacher. Why tell stories? According to Gary Zustiak in his book *The Next Generation,* "A good story conveys a truth to the listener because it provides . . . a picture of reality. [Good stories] allow people the chance to reflect upon their own life experiences and find answers to their own problems" (Zustiak 1996). In other words, students see their own lives as they reflect on the lives of others. Our students desperately need to see and hear how others are living out their Christianity. Before they will be willing to trust God with their lives, they need to see that God is working in other peoples' lives.

> We need to bring students to a place where God's Story intersects with their stories.

A gripping example of the power of God's Story is found in the film *Amistad.* This film tells the story of a group of Africans who are captured by slave traders and loaded onto a ship headed for America where they are to be sold as slaves. In an effort to free themselves, the slaves overpower and kill the crew.

The slaves are eventually recaptured and taken to America to stand trial for murder. They are thrown into prison to await their trial and expected execution. While in prison, the slaves are given a Bible. Although the slaves cannot speak or read English, this Bible has pictures in it of the life of Christ.

One night one of the slaves, Yamba, is reading the Bible when another slave comments, "You don't have to pretend to understand. It's just us now." Yamba replies, "I think I do understand the story. Come see."

Yamba shows the pictures to the second slave, explaining the story of the birth, life, death, and resurrection of Jesus Christ. At one point the second slave interrupts and says, "But it's only a *story.*" Yamba doesn't accept this; he now sees it as *his* story. Toward the end of his conversation, Yamba points to a picture of Jesus ascending to heaven and says, "This is where the soul goes when you die. This is where we are going when they kill us. It doesn't look too bad."

Yamba discovered hope by looking at the Bible and understanding the story of redemption. He found his story in the Story of God. As teachers of God's Word (or tellers of God's Story), we can tell our students, "There *is* a grand Story that makes sense of all your stories, a Story that brings meaning to your life." We need to bring students to a place where God's Story intersects with their stories—where they can finally experience God in a way that makes sense to them. That is the purpose of this book. Let's discover what this means in the next chapter.

CHAPTER 2

PARTICIPATING

IN THE STORY

OF GOD:

A NARRATIVE

UNDERSTANDING

OF CHRISTIAN

MINISTRY

TIM GREEN

Pointing to the large pile of stones gathered near the river, a young teen asks her grandmother, "Why are those rocks there?" Having waited for that very question to be asked, the teen's trusted mentor answers, "It's an amazing story—one that I heard over and over again as I was growing up. Many years ago, our ancestors were slaves in Egypt, but the Lord

...ught us out of Egypt with a mighty hand. . . ." The grandmother continues by recounting the way in which God called a leader, plagues struck the Egyptians, waters were divided, manna was provided, and a covenant was made.

In another corner of the village, several persons have gathered around the evening fire, singing songs and recounting the amazing exploits and sincere faith of ancestors such as Deborah, Gideon, Hannah, and David. Some around the fire have heard these stories dozens of times. For others in the circle, this night is one of initiation as they hear of events and experiences that will define their identity and shape their character for the remainder of their lives.

> **Piece by piece, through stories, songs, sermons, and letters, the kingdom of God is consistently and deliberately handed to the next generation.**

The conversation between the young teen and her grandmother, as well as the dialogue around the community campfire, is a snapshot of what the people of God have been doing for thousands of years. Throughout our history, the faith, like a baton in a relay race, has been passed on from one generation to the next. Recounting what God has done in the life of His community, the people of God have creatively invited the next generation to become active participants in God's ongoing activity, whether it be through piling stones, telling stories, singing songs, preaching sermons, writing letters, or celebrating central events around a meal. They faithfully carried out the ancient task given to subsequent generations: "Recite them to your children and talk about them when you are at home and when you are away, when you lie down and when you rise, bind them as a sign on your hand, fix them as an emblem on your forehead, and write them on the doorposts of your house and on your gates" (Deut. 6:7-9).

Now, thousands of years later, we face the same challenge that all generations before us have faced: how are we to pass the ancient faith to the next generation? Increasingly, since the days of the Enlightenment in the 18th century, we have all too easily become satisfied with reducing the work of God to a list of points or propositions that can then be applied to life. Like a winepress, we tend to "squeeze the juice" out of biblical stories, songs, and letters, reducing them to a set of "how-tos" or "applicable points." We then give those reductions to our students as simple ways to make it through another week. The problem is that nothing is left of the story, the song, or the letter. As a result, God's past and present activity becomes distant and foreign to our lives. Scripture becomes nothing more than a how-to manual or a rule book, and the Church is perceived as an antiquated way of dealing with life or an over-bearing authority figure.

Likewise, our students are never challenged to think about their faith *within* the story, the song, or the letter; everything is done for them. As a result, the life of faith can quickly become a mindless and heartless following of points rather than a transformed way of thinking and being in the world.

Furthermore, even when biblical truths are applied to the dominant culture in which we live, that dominant culture often continues to deter-mine our priorities. We may provide our students with a few biblical steps for surviving in the *real* world and offer lifestyles to guarantee eternal life, but our own identity and the identities of our students continue to be shaped by the dominant culture. The kingdom of God as it is depicted in Scripture and the subsequent history of the Church becomes nothing more than a foreign object to observe rather than a home in which to live.

One of our greatest challenges is to rediscover and practice the man-ner in which our ancestors have consistently communicated the faith and talked about God. Our spiritual ancestors challenge us to do something other than give our students spiritual how-tos. We must speak of an alter-native world within which to live, a lens through which life can be seen and understood, and an identity that will shape character and lifestyle.

How might we face the challenge that confronts us? The Story of God and His people has already provided an answer to that very question. Piece by piece, stories, songs, sermons, letters, creeds, holidays, and sacra-ments, all belonging to a counterkingdom, the kingdom of God, are consis-tently and deliberately handed to the next generation. Out of those numer-ous pieces is constructed an alternative world in which our students can find their identity and their character.

25

More than simply telling numerous disconnected stories, we recognize that for the people of God there exists one grand narrative, beginning with the earliest chapters of the Bible and extending through the history of the Christian Church down to the present day. It is a *megastory* with a grand plot: God is reconciling the world to himself through His people. In more recent years, such an approach to ministry that calls persons to find their identity *within* the grand Story of God has been given the name *narrative*. Although the name may be a recent development, the method of inviting subsequent generations to participate in the *megastory* of God, to discover their identity within that Story, and to develop a character in light of that identity has deep roots in Scripture and Christian tradition. Such an approach to ministry and discipleship has been the distinctive way in which the people of God have talked about God. We might call this way of talking about God *narrative theology*.

As teachers, mentors, parents, and youth workers, what would it mean for *us* to practice ministry as "narrative God-talkers"? What would it mean for *us* to understand our own identity as being *narrative theologians*? Certainly, all of us who talk about God, His nature, His activity among us, and His will for our lives, whether it be in messages, Bible studies, or counseling sessions, are God-talkers (theologians). The question for us is never "*Are* we theologians?" Rather, as persons whose primary responsibility is to speak about God and name His activity in the lives of students, the question is "*What type* of theologians are we?" As we step into the world of narrative, let us explore what it would mean for us to practice youth ministry as narrative God-talkers.

Narrative God-Talkers Recognize the Powerful Role of Language

Throughout our history, the people of God have understood and appreciated the powerful nature of language, whether spoken, sung, or nonverbal. As a culture that spans all ethnic, racial, and gender groups, Kingdom-culture has always had a peculiar language—a language of grace rather than achievement, hope rather than despair, wholeness rather than brokenness, and self-giving love rather than self-serving power. This language seldom "fits" into the dominant world culture; rather it stands in sharp contrast to that culture.

Because words and symbols have an amazingly creative power, narrative God-talkers carefully choose meaningful ways to speak about God to students. The words we speak shape a world in which students will find their identity and will eventually view all of life. Therefore, we select words that are deliberate and purposeful. Because we understand the powerful and creative nature of words, the language we use in messages, songs, Bible studies, and counseling sessions is always purposeful and consistent with what it means to be Kingdom-culture people.

As specific words and phrases are often repeated, they become signs of our connectedness to God and to each other when we gather and reminders of our identity when we scatter. Therefore, we deliberately develop a vocabulary in which we communicate and celebrate who we are. As we come together, we frequently join our voices in the well-known Kingdom prayer that Jesus taught His disciples, and we recite commonly known ancient confessions. By doing this, we recall *who* we are as well as the *connectedness* we share with each other and with those who came before us.

Rather than a vocabulary of exclusiveness that keeps outsiders on the outside, the very nature of the language we use invites others to become active participants as well. Prayers, confessions, phrases of identification, and songs are never intended to be secret, hidden "code words" for insiders. Instead, our words and actions are always carried out so that new members might readily be accepted into the Kingdom-culture. At the same time, however, the people of God do not refrain from the unique language of the Kingdom under the guise of inclusiveness. Simply adapting the language and symbols of the dominant culture at the expense of Kingdom-culture compromises the uniqueness of this Kingdom. For the people of God, Kingdom-culture never becomes overshadowed and hidden by the language, symbols, priorities, and values of the dominant culture in which we live.

Just as we recognize the creative power of spoken language, the people of God have also understood and celebrated the power of nonverbal communication. Whether it be a pile of stones, a stained-glass window, a cross, or a poster, the people of God have always sought creatively to place nonverbal symbols in front of their young, anticipating those teaching moments when the question is raised, "What do those mean?" Rather than being forms of alienation or keeping "outsiders" out, these symbols have always been understood as forms of invitation and incorporation.

As we can see, narrative God-talkers are keenly aware of the central role of language in ministry. We recognize that the words we speak, the songs we sing, and the symbols we use do not merely testify to what God has done sometime in the past; they also point forward to a world, a Kingdom-culture, in which we are called to live. Certainly, testimonies of *what God has done* lead us to anticipate *what God will do.* Through their words, teachers, Bible study leaders, mentors, parents, youth workers, and pastors accept the great privilege and responsibility of participating in God's ongoing activity of creating a Kingdom in which we reside.

Narrative God-Talkers Speak of an "Alternative World"

At the heart of being a narrative God-talker is the understanding that this language we use ultimately speaks of another world, even another *culture.* As the writer to the Hebrews (chapter 11) clearly understood, we also embrace the reality that we are "strangers and foreigners on the earth." While we reside in this world, our "citizenship" belongs to another Kingdom. We live within Kingdom-culture, and every time we engage in ministry with our students, they are becoming accepted into that Kingdom-culture.

Under the legitimate name of evangelism, we can all too easily succumb to the temptation to "package" the kingdom of God in the language and values of our society's dominant culture. However, Kingdom-culture is not simply a survival tactic for living in our dominant culture, but rather, it is a whole other way of *being.* That is why we boldly call our young people to find their identity, their values, their language, their priorities, even their very existence within this unique alternative Kingdom.

At the same time, narrative God-talkers recognize that living in Kingdom-culture is not a matter of alienating or even withdrawing ourselves from the world in which we live. Indeed, Jesus himself did not pray that His followers be removed from the dominant culture, but that we be protected from its evil power (John 17:15). Discovering our true identity and very existence *within* the alternative world of the kingdom of God, the people of God then step back into the world and dominant culture. However, we step into that world with "Kingdom lenses." Life in the dominant culture, with all of its relationships, decisions, and dreams, is then viewed from the perspective of the Kingdom.

Narrative God-Talkers Emphasize Participation

After we discover that we are citizens of this alternative world, this Kingdom-culture, we will come to realize that we are not merely observers of an ancient event; we are participants in a present event. A narrative God-talker will invite students to come down from the "spectator's balcony" and to step onto the stage, thereby becoming a part of the great drama itself. As students find themselves living within the Kingdom-culture, they will recognize that they are participants in something much larger than themselves. They are presently a part of the great drama of God!

Such participation provides a sense of connectedness, not only to other persons who are presently citizens of this Kingdom, but also to all of those persons who have come before and to all of those who will follow. Students come to recognize and celebrate that they have been *caught up* in something that extends in time far beyond themselves. This Kingdom is not simply a new fad that has recently dropped out of the sky. Therefore, rather than rejecting tradition, students celebrate that their very identities are found within the greater context of that tradition. They are intricately *connected* to what has come before!

Not only does such participation provide connectedness to persons of other times, but it also provides connectedness to persons of other locations. Rather than being suspicious of other ethnic, racial, or language groups, our students celebrate their differences within a Kingdom that knows no ethnic, racial, language, or gender boundaries. We are *connected* around the globe!

One of the most consistent ways in which the people of God have celebrated and made visible their participation in the Kingdom-culture is by marking time in a unique way. From our earliest ancestors, we have lived our lives according to special days, seasons, and times. Our Hebrew ancestors marked time according to God's great acts at the Red Sea (Passover and Unleavened Bread), at Mount Sinai (Festival of Weeks/Pentecost), and in the wilderness (Festival of Tabernacles). Early on, our Christian ancestors began to mark time according to the events in the life of Jesus. All we have ever known as the people of God is to mark time according to the great activities of God in the life of His people. One tool to help us with marking this time is the Christian calendar. (See Appendix A for a brief overview of why we use the Christian calendar and Appendix B for an overview of the seasons and themes of the Christian calendar.)

As our young people are encouraged to order their lives according to time as shown by the Christian calendar, they increasingly come to understand the meaning of participation *in Christ*. Kingdom-culture is heard, seen, felt, tasted, and known as they creatively participate in the great events of the anticipation, birth, life, suffering, death, resurrection, and ascension of Jesus Christ.

Therefore, the call to active participation provides connectedness not only to other persons across space and time but ultimately to what God himself has been and is doing. Being caught up "in Christ," the people of God come to recognize, appreciate, and celebrate that we are *literally* participants in the ministry and work of God on earth. Rather than a student discovering *his or her* own ministry, he or she comes to discover his or her unique place *within* the ministry of Jesus Christ as He continues to carry out His work in the world. Rather than God simply coming *into* the individual student, the individual student realizes and celebrates that he or she is being caught up *in Christ* himself and in the ministry of Christ.

Narrative God-Talkers Seek Community Formation

As students become active participants in something larger than themselves, they will soon discover that they have become part of a group of people that extends far beyond themselves. They have become a part of a community. Having abandoned the spectator stands where individualism runs rampant, students step onto a stage and into a story where deciding whether or not to share life with other characters is not even an option. No monologues occur on this stage! Community is essential. Narrative God-talkers particularly appreciate the need for authentic community formation. From programs that are planned to messages that are given, from songs that are sung to ministry opportunities that are provided, our language and actions will reflect the central conviction that God has always been creating and continues to create a people, not isolated superheroes! The language of *I, me,* and *my* will give way to the language of *we, us,* and *our*. Certainly, the place of the individual is not rejected, but it is viewed in relationship to the entire body (1 Cor. 12:27). Students will come to see themselves in relation to the grand community to which they belong.

Throughout the history of the people of God, this authentic community has consisted of both peers and mentors. A youth ministry that invites students to participate in Kingdom life will seek to connect them to both peers and mentors. On the one hand, persons who share common joys, fears, dreams, and disappointments will have the opportunity to celebrate, grieve, pray, learn, and dream together. Gatherings of celebration, worship, study, and accountability will intentionally connect students to their peers.

On the other hand, trusted and experienced persons who can "point to the stories" and describe their meaning have always been invaluable members of the people of God. These persons are no less significant today. We can and should provide opportunities for students to share life with women and men who witness to the faithfulness of God in the joys, fears, dreams, and disappointments of their journeys.

Narrative God-Talkers Are Committed to Identity Formation

As we participate in the Kingdom-culture and as we discover our connectedness to persons across all space and time, all of life begins to be viewed against the backdrop of this Kingdom. Particularly, our very identity is transformed as we see ourselves in light of the Kingdom community in which we live.

The Kingdom-story begins to shape us. Stories of our origins, our struggles, our victories, and our future begin to mold every aspect of who we are. Rather than measuring our identity according to the yardstick that the dominant culture uses, we increasingly see ourselves in relationship to this Kingdom. Kingdom priorities begin to inform our decisions. Kingdom values begin to shape our relationships. And Kingdom hopes begin to mold our dreams.

Narrative God-talkers recognize that the formation of a student's identity itself is at stake. The language that we are using, the Kingdom-culture that we are demonstrating, and the community that we are a part of will provide the backdrop against which our students will come to understand who they are. No doubt, just as the people of God have always had ongoing competition, so will we. The industries and media of our dominant culture have a great deal at stake in shaping the identity of our students. However, we are called to the same boldness and integrity that the people of God have always demonstrated in speaking of another Kingdom. Without apology, narrative God-talkers speak of a whole other way of *being* in this world.

Narrative God-Talkers View
Character Formation as the Fruit of Identity

As identity is shaped, character and lifestyle emerge. From the preface to the Ten Commandments (Exod. 20:2) to the outset of the Sermon on the Mount (Matt. 5:1-16), the people of God have consistently recognized that our way of living is the direct result of *who* we are. And who we are is always the direct result of what God has graciously caused us to be. As narrative God-talkers, we do not seek to moralize or heap disconnected rules upon students. Rather, by inviting students to see themselves and others *within* the Story of God, we provide the setting wherein authentic character and ethic can develop and grow. As a result, lifestyle becomes a genuine fruit of identity. The life of holiness is then viewed not as what makes our students holy, but as the result of God's gracious, mind-transforming work in their lives. The answer to the question, "What are we to do?" emerges out of the answer to the question, "Who are we?" As a result, when students confront new moral dilemmas or situations, the Kingdom-identity being shaped in their lives will inform their decisions.

Narrative God-Talkers See the Whole

As much as we would like to provide our students with everything they need for the journey in one retreat, one Bible study, or one worship experience, or as much as we would wish to summarize everything for our youth group in one cliché, one scripture verse, or one song, the Story of God paints a very different picture for us. The people of God have always been committed to *the whole*. In spite of living in a dominant culture of rapid remedies and quick fixes, fast food and instant gratification, we belong to the Kingdom-culture, which views life as a journey, comprised of many steps and stages.

> We face the great challenge of passing the faith on to the next generation.

The characters with whom we share life and ministry were not men and women who went into a situation briefly and made a big splash, thus solving all the problems and answering all the questions. Instead, they were men and women who were committed to the long haul. They neither gave up when mountaintops of victory disintegrated, nor did they run away when great battles erupted in the valley. They stayed, they persisted, they continued! Why? They knew that the Story of God was not something that they must complete in a day, a month, or a year. It was greater than any one single victory; it was stronger than any multitude of defeats. And ultimately, it wasn't their story anyway—it was God's!

As narrative God-talkers, we also are committed to the *whole*. We recognize that no single verse in Scripture will provide the final answer. Instead, we are committed to the full canon of Scripture. Therefore, we allow verse after verse, passage after passage, book after book to dialogue with all of the others. We allow the pleasant and simple passages of Scripture to be read, taught, and explored right alongside the more unpleasant and complex passages. As narrative God-talkers, we are not quick to make one passage fit another, but we allow Bible passages to stand side by side, and thus permit our students to see the *whole*, not only one *piece*.

Just as we are committed to the *whole* of Scripture, we are also committed to the *whole* of spiritual formation. For individual students, as well as for an entire class, we recognize and celebrate the fact that spiritual development is an ongoing process. It began before we ever stepped into our students' lives, and it will continue far beyond our immediate ministry with them. Rather than basing all ministry upon what magnificent accomplishments can quickly be achieved, narrative God-talkers view spiritual formation from a much larger perspective. We are committed to providing students with one passage at a time, one song at a time, and one prayer at a time. We know that the God who has called us into His ministry will ultimately bring the many pieces together into a *whole*—a *whole* that extends far beyond the years of adolescence.

At the same time, we recognize the significance of every time we get together and "God-talk" with a student, whether it be after school over a soft drink, at a campground for fall retreat, in a home for an afterglow, on Wednesday evening for worship, or around the circle for Bible study. We realize that every word we speak, every song we sing, and every silent symbol we view places one more stitch into the fabric of our students' spiritual formation.

Narrative God-Talk and Youth Ministry

Like every generation that has come before us, we face the great challenge of passing the faith on to the next generation. How are we to face this challenge with integrity and faithfulness? Our story already tells us how to communicate the truth of the Scriptures: "Recite them to your children and talk about them when you are at home and when you are away, when you lie down and when you rise. Bind them as a sign on your hand, fix them as an emblem on your forehead, and write them on the doorposts of your house and on your gates" (Deut. 6:7-9, NRSV).

We face the challenge by being God-talkers, even theologians, who name God in the world of our students! How do we legitimately speak of God? Recognizing the creative power of language, we confidently and creatively articulate this alternative Kingdom, this Kingdom-culture, in such a way that our students actively participate in the community of God's people, where they discover their true identity. Perhaps no greater calling is to be found than the calling to be a God-talker as we anticipate the question, "Why are those rocks there?"

HAPTER 3

TEACHING

FOR A

LIFETIME

RICK EDWARDS

Adolescence is typically considered an "in-between" stage of life. Some observers have described teenagers as no longer children, but not yet adults. This view seems a bit pessimistic, for it describes adolescence in terms of what is lacking. It leaves the impression that students live in one big vacuum, devoid of meaning, joy, or significance. Perhaps we should instead think of our students as *both* children and adults. To be sure, this mix of childlike and adult attitudes and behaviors can be chaotic and confusing—to their parents, teachers, and youth workers, but also to students themselves. Even so, research tells us that for the large majority of teenagers, adolescence is also an exciting time of growth and creativity, as teenagers learn new things about themselves, the world, and God (Kipke 1995). This chapter will explore some of the dynamics that occur during adolescence in the area of faith development.

Faith development in teenagers is not an oxymoron; they are quite capable of growing and maturing in their faith, just as they do in their bodies, minds, and social skills. However, strong, healthy faith is not automatic or guaranteed. Too many teachers have witnessed the tragedy of young teens or new converts who regularly attend Sunday School classes and youth group events, but gradually stop coming, and even in some cases, choose not to follow Christ any longer (DeVries 1994).[1] What causes this pattern, and what can we do to help our students keep a lifelong commitment to Christ and His Church?

We can point to sports, music, and work as competitors for our students' time and energy. To some degree we would be correct in doing so. However, these outside influences and distractions may not be the main culprits. In his book *Family-Based Youth Ministry,* youth worker Mark DeVries identifies a subtle, but more dangerous problem: our own youth ministries—or more precisely, our goals for youth ministry (1994). We aim to make mature Christian teenagers who regularly attend youth events, Christians who say and do all the right things. But DeVries says this goal is shortsighted, for adolescent faith is different from adult faith and cannot hold up to the challenges of adulthood.

We should aim instead at building in our students a lasting Christian identity that will enable our students to become mature Christian *adults.* "If we gain nothing else from adolescence, we must obtain a coherent sense of self, or 'identity,' to navigate future life stages successfully" (Dean and Foster 1998). Mature Christian adults are less likely to abandon their faith because it lies at the core of their identities.

What Is a Mature Christian Adult?

If the long-range goal of our youth ministry and teaching is to create mature Christian adults, we need to know what such a person looks like. In his book *On the Way,* Christian educator Les Steele offers some general descriptions of mature Christians. Maturing Christians' identities are centered on the gospel (1990). Maturing Christians can also observe and reflect on their own thoughts and actions and compare those with the claims of the gospel. They also recognize that life is complex and can live with questions that have no satisfactory answers (such as, "Why do innocent people suffer?"). Even though mature Christian adults have a firm sense of self, they are not self-centered; to the contrary, they focus on glorifying God and doing His will. They also have a healthy concern for others and accept people warmly and build healthy relationships with them. Maturing Christians realize that they were created for relationships and that the faith community is the best place for them to mature, learn about and experience God, and to minister to others.

These are broad, general ideas of what a mature Christian adult is like. A more specific description comes from in-depth research of various Protestant congregations (Search Institute 1990). The researchers designed an inventory that measured faith maturity of teenagers and adults. They found that people who have a mature Christian faith:

- Trust and believe in God and accept the divinity and humanity of Jesus.
- Accept God's love as unconditional, not based on human works or merit.
- Experience God's guidance in daily life.
- Feel set free and have a sense of peace, meaning, and purpose in life.
- Have a strong sense of self-esteem and acceptance.
- Integrate their faith into daily life by basing their morals, daily decisions, and actions (including political and social actions) on their personal faith in Jesus.
- Realize that faith is a journey that requires change and growth.
- Seek spiritual growth by studying the Bible and by engaging in private prayer and other opportunities for spiritual growth.
- Develop their faith and that of others, especially by sharing faith stories and encountering God together through various acts of worship.
- Hold life-affirming values, which affect their personal lifestyle and acceptance of other people as equals.
- Support social justice efforts that reduce poverty and improve human welfare, including devoting their own time, money, and energy in acts of compassion.

We should emphasize two things about these descriptions, the first being that these are highly idealistic. It's doubtful any of your students meet all the characteristics listed. In fact, not many adults would fill all the descriptions perfectly. Even so, these descriptions give us a goal for our teaching ministry. (Appendix A contains a survey you can use to identify your own level of faith maturity; you may want to adapt the language and use it with your students.)

Second, remember that these descriptions are not a checklist of behaviors we can train our students to exhibit. These marks of mature faith flow from one's core identity. They are the natural results of an inner quality that lies beyond our ability to create.

Nurturing Christian Adulthood

Even though we cannot simply manufacture mature Christian adults, there are some things we can do to influence, direct, and nurture the process in our students. But we can't do it alone; it requires cooperation. The Carnegie Council on Adolescent Development and the National Academy of Science found that healthy adolescent development must involve a variety of social institutions: families, schools, health-care systems, and community organizations, including religious organizations.

In the same regard, it takes several influences to develop a strong, lasting faith. A research study discovered that people who remained involved in church past their teen years shared the following six characteristics, listed here in order of importance/influence:[2]

1. Faith is integrated into family identity and practice. This means that children and teens grow up in families where faith is understood as part of family life, including daily, weekly, and annual routines and traditions. They understand that to be a Smith (for example) is to be a Christian.

2. Students have regular access to three or more adult mentors who model their faith. These mentors are persons other than father or mother, such as grandparents, aunts or uncles, pastors, Sunday School teachers, youth workers, and so on.

3. Students are involved in service to the world. These opportunities may be simple volunteer work for neighbors or formal mission trip experiences.

4. Students take part in apprenticeship opportunities. These may be official training in some sort of trade or may be informal training and practice in some skill at church or other community organizations.

5. Students belong to supportive, relevant, engaging congregations. Congregations can support students by providing people and financial resources for youth ministry. Congregations are relevant if they are aware of youth culture trends and seek to use culturally appropriate methods to communicate with students. Congregations can engage students by allowing them to fully participate in all aspects of congregational life, rather than allowing them to become a separate "church within a church."

6. Churches provide excellent youth ministries.

Take note of the first five factors: they rely on human resources rather than on money, and on personal relationships more than programs. This means that churches of nearly any size can provide the essential elements for lasting faith development. As Dean and Foster put it, "Significant relationships with Christians are crucial if we stand any chance of forming an identity that takes into account who we are in God's eyes" (1998).

This research makes it clear that family and congregation working together have a powerful influence on the formation of a lasting Christian identity. This identity shapes students' attitudes, beliefs, and behaviors in ways that last well past adolescence. Such deep-seated identity becomes part of the individual's life story.

> As people meet God, their life stories, even their very identities, are shaped.

Christian Identity and Life Story

This talk of relationships in family and congregation, identity development, and life story calls to mind the discussion of narrative theology in chapter 2. Each person's identity is shaped by previous life experiences, primarily relationships with family members, friends, and, for Christians, by relationships with their congregation. All these entities have their own stories, their histories that feature key people and crucial events. As individuals develop their identities, they integrate these family and congregational stories into their personal stories. Or, to put it the other way around, individuals join themselves to the stories of their families and churches, which existed prior to any one individual.

As narrative theology reminds us, the stories in the Bible form one large, overarching Story, in which God is the main character and actor. As people meet God, their life stories, even their very identities, are shaped (or reshaped). The stories of key biblical characters demonstrate this when their names were changed after significant encounters with God (names carried great symbolic meaning in those cultures). For example, after God promised Abram ("exalted father") and Sarai ("princess") a child and many descendants, He also gave them new names: Abraham ("father of many") and Sarah ("mother of many"). Jacob ("heel-grabber") became Israel ("he struggles with God") after his wrestling match at the ford of Jabbok. The Jewish persecutor of the Early Church, Saul, met the risen Christ on the road to Damascus. Shortly afterward, Saul was given the typical Roman name of Paul, to match his new mission in life: to take the gospel to the Gentiles.

As our students' Christian identities develop, they will join themselves to God's Story, adopt it as their own, and find their role in it as the Story continues to unfold in history. God may not change their names, but just as He did for their ancestors in the faith, He will draw them, along with their personal stories and identities, into His larger Story.

Mature Christian Faith

As our students' identity develops and they grow toward mature Christian adulthood, their faith will undergo significant changes (encounters with the Creator of the universe tend to leave an effect or two!). In order to teach our students effectively, we need to understand some of the details of this process. When we recognize the signs of growth in our students, we can adjust our teaching accordingly.

We will use a model of faith summarized by Christian educator Les Steele. Steele defines faith as "human response to God's redemption" (1990). God takes the initiative, inviting us to accept His forgiveness and new life made possible through the life, death, and resurrection of Jesus. We respond by accepting God's offer and allowing His grace to change us. This human side of faith has three interrelated aspects: belief, behavior, and attitude.

Faith as Belief

The act of believing is a mental aspect of faith, for it is a function of the mind. As our students grow in faith, they will begin thinking in new ways about God. This is directly related to their developing ability to think about abstract concepts. They are capable of considering the mysteries of God and salvation, such as the Trinity, the humanity and divinity of Christ, and the problem of evil, to name just a few. They can now understand and appreciate the symbolism and rich meanings of the biblical stories they learned in childhood. Our students can now see themselves *in* the story of faith, rather than just knowing the facts of the story.

Faith as belief not only concerns the process of believing but also has to do with the content of one's beliefs. (It is like the difference between a computer's operating system on one hand, and the documents or data stored and used on the other hand.) Right beliefs about God will have a domino effect on the rest of our beliefs about Jesus, sin, human nature, salvation, and ethical living. The Church has a rich history of people who have thought long and hard about doctrinal issues. Our job as teachers is to know at least the basics of theology and communicate them accurately to our students.

In doing so, there are two extremes we will want to avoid. The first is to overemphasize minor points of doctrine at the expense of personal relationships. Wars have been fought, people have been burned at the stake, and congregations have split into pieces because of slight differences in biblical interpretation or theological definitions. Besides hurting fellow Christians, such behavior damages our witness to nonbelievers. For a mature Christian, Christian unity is more important than minor points of theological correctness.

The other extreme we should avoid lies in the opposite direction; that is to ignore or disrespect our own faith community's story and doctrinal distinctives. This error often is expressed in statements such as, "I don't push church membership on my students; it's enough for them just to be good Christians." The problem with this thinking is that there is no such thing as a generic Christian. Everyone has his or her own particular opinions or beliefs on sacraments, conversion, the Holy Spirit, the Atonement, and so on, which will differ at some point from someone else's.

This truth is built into the theology of Incarnation: The Christian story is not about just any man; Jesus of Nazareth was born into a specific family in a certain country, and spoke in a particular language with a distinctive accent, and He looked like no one else. God has always worked in specific ways with particular people.

In the same way, we live in a particular "chapter" of God's Story. We do a disservice to our ancestors in the faith, as well to our students, if we do not encourage them to join us. This is not to say that we should confine our ministry to our local congregation or only our denomination's programs. Partnerships with other denominations can still thrive when we unite on the common elements of the faith, while respecting each others' distinctive beliefs and traditions.

Faith as Behavior

A second aspect of faith is behavior (or practice), which is carried out in the physical realm. We are called to do what God commands us. Jesus, Paul, and James all emphasized the importance of acting on one's beliefs. Good deeds must come from good theology, just as good theology will result in good deeds. Faith as behavior asks, "What does it mean to build the kingdom of God, and what does it look like in our contemporary society?" It may be more helpful to encourage our students to look for what God is doing in the world and join that effort, rather than trying to create new programs, service projects, evangelistic efforts, and so on.

Christian behavior operates in the world on three levels: the personal, the interpersonal, and the social. The personal level calls us to bring our life into closer likeness to the image of Christ. We can teach our students how to practice the inner spiritual disciplines of prayer, Bible study, fasting, silence, contemplation, and so on.

The interpersonal level of Christian behavior is where we learn to treat others with holy love, respect, and mercy. Christian ethics call us to rely on God as we develop honesty and purity, along with all the other Christian virtues.

The social level of Christian behavior challenges our faith to work in the larger systems and structures of the world. The kingdom of God can make its way into the social, political, cultural, and environmental arenas and redeem them. We can help our students develop at this level by involving them in service and mission opportunities, both near to home and far away.

Faith as Attitude

Faith as attitude deals in the realm of the emotions, passions, desires, and motives. The emotion related most closely to faith is trust. Only when we trust God are we likely to place our lives in His hands and make His kingdom the destination of our life journey. This kind of trust doesn't just happen; it grows out of past experience with those who have positions of power and responsibility for us (such as parents, teachers, and pastors). At some point, we take the risk of initially trusting God. From there on, our trust deepens enough that we can surrender our wills and ourselves to God as we experience His faithfulness to us.

This, in turn, teaches us how to be faithful, both to God and to other people. We are called to persevere in the faith, to stick with it, even when we have doubts or hard times. Furthermore, as the quality of faithfulness develops in us, our emotional lives become redeemed. Mature faith is less and less subject to the ups and downs of our natural emotions. Instead, we become motivated by purer degrees of love for God and for our neighbor. We become more stable and consistent in our commitment to God and in our relationships with other people.

We may not notice this much in our students, for during adolescence the emotions are affected by sudden doses of strong hormones. Nevertheless, our calm and steady behavior can serve as good examples of faith and as sources of comfort for our students in their times of distress.

Implications for Teaching

It might appear upon first reading of this chapter that we who are mere teachers and youth workers are in way over our heads. We are dealing with students who are influenced by powerful forces like family dynamics, puberty, peer pressure, identity crises, faith development, and so on. What impact can we make? Our time, energy, and resources are limited. Besides, we have access to our students only once or twice a week for an hour at a time. What good does our teaching do in the face of all the voices and activities our students experience? Why not just have some socials and an occasional Coke or two and save this business of "faith development" for a concentrated time of spiritual emphasis like retreats, summer camps, or revivals?

In response to these questions and doubts, we have to admit we *are* in over our heads, out of our league, between a rock and a hard place, all at the same time. But that's OK, because identity formation and faith development is God's work, not ours. Although this chapter has explored what we can do for our students, we must understand that teachers merely set the mood and environment for faith development; it's God who brings the growth.

Furthermore, we have to admit that teaching is a rather humble task. Studies have shown that the most powerful and memorable spiritual experiences are retreats, camps, revivals, mission trips, and other "big" events. A good youth ministry will include some of these opportunities. However, as Dean and Foster point out, big events have their own limitations: "Mountaintop experiences represent needed kerosene thrown onto sluggish faith, but kerosene alone cannot keep a fire alive" (1998). A good, lasting fire needs plain old tinder, kindling, and logs. Your teaching, in weekly classes, Bible studies, and youth meetings supplies the fuel that is necessary for consistent growth.

Another hint to the value of teaching is seen in the example of Jesus himself. Sure, He calmed storms, fed thousands with one boy's lunch, and performed many other amazing feats, but He also served through the humble, yet honorable task of teaching. He taught in all sorts of situations. He talked with people one-on-one; He told stories in small groups; He taught large crowds. We should not underestimate the power and long-lasting effects of teaching.

Having acknowledged the proper role of teaching, let's look at what we can do to lead our students toward mature Christian adulthood. The task is great, but just as one eats the proverbial elephant one bite at a time, it can be done by starting with a few small steps.

Build Relationships

We have seen that a mature faith is formed in the context of personal relationships, especially intergenerational relationships. Mark DeVries makes this point forcefully: "Teenagers will not learn the skills required of mature adults in a peer-centered youth Sunday-School class. They will not learn these skills by talking with their friends. The process occurs as the less mature repeatedly have the opportunity to observe, dialogue and collaborate with the more mature" (1994). Work hard at developing good relationships with your students. Spend time with them outside of class.

Call or send notes on their birthdays, before big games or concerts, or just to say "hi" and remind them that you are praying for them. For more details about the nature of the teacher-student relationship, read chapter 4.

You can also help them develop relationships with other adults in the congregation. Find ways of bringing adults into your classroom, perhaps as members of a discussion panel. Have adults from your congregation visit your class on occasion to tell their stories of faith. Have them serve as mentors, small-group discussion leaders, or even teaching assistants—anything to get more students connected to more adults. When students hear adults' faith stories and see adults as examples of faithful living, they will be encouraged that the Christian life is possible and worthwhile. "The appearance of someone who has already taken the journey can bring a sigh of relief to the best of us" (Daloz 1987).

Invite Students into God's Story

We have seen that Christian identity is formed in our students when they join their individual stories to God's overarching Story. This process occurs as students participate in the life of the congregation as it recalls and reenacts in worship God's great acts of redemption. It occurs when students meet the needs of others.

Teach your students how to practice these acts of faith. Explain what true worship is, what sacraments are, how and why we pray. Discuss the relationship of faith and good deeds and how to find the right balance of each. Teach by doing: lead your students in acts of compassion to nonbelievers and in ministry in the congregation. Explore the beliefs that lie behind all these practices so students will know why we do what we do.

Teaching these and the many other topics your students need to know requires a reliable method. It is best to begin your teaching sessions by allowing your students to share and examine their experiences and understanding of the lesson topic. Then you can lead them to explore God's Story—what is His perspective and how have His people responded to the issue? Knowing God's Story is not the end, though. You must next help your students catch a vision of what life would be like if they were to join themselves to what God is doing in the world. Invite them to enter God's Story and become part of the next episode. Chapter 5 of this book describes a teaching model for doing this very thing.

Teach for Holistic Faith

We found that faith is comprised of three interrelated aspects: belief, behavior, and attitude, each of which has various components. Our job is to help our students develop a well-rounded, holistic faith that builds these various components of faith. Therefore, our teaching methods should target different aspects of faith. Lessons on beliefs will benefit from careful explanations and perhaps some object lessons to illustrate abstract concepts, such as the Trinity. Lessons on Christian behavior (such as prayer or servanthood) will be most effective if we provide opportunity to practice each behavior. Case studies or actual participation would be appropriate. Lessons on matters of attitude can make use of stories or rituals that touch the heart and emotions (without being manipulative). The authentic testimony of another person, a well-written story, or appropriate video clips can all have powerful effects on students' attitudes and motives.

Developing holistic faith through teaching also requires us to use methods that are appropriate for our students. Just as students have different personalities (such as introvert or extrovert), they also have different learning styles. You will need to take into account your students' learning styles as you select teaching methods that meet the needs of each student. Read chapter 6 for more details on learning styles and teaching methods.

Following these guidelines (and the more detailed explanations in chapters 4, 5, and 6) will help your congregation guide your students along the path to mature Christian faith. Dean and Foster remind us of the importance of a community of believers that provides a safe place to belong and learn: "Youth instinctively seek such communities as they pull away from traditional authority figures. In the absence of a sanctioned extended family like a congregation, youth will adopt a substitute—and it's worth remembering that the surrogate families of gangs, peer groups, cults, and 'virtual' communities over the Internet often welcome adolescents more readily than the church" (1998).

As you lead your students on the journey toward mature Christian adulthood, may you be aware of the presence of a fellow traveler who has already blazed the trail, but who finds no greater joy than in walking alongside His followers.

CHAPTER 4

UNDERSTANDING

YOUR ROLE

AS A

GUIDE

MARK HAYSE

The Best of the Bunch

When does a good teacher become a favorite teacher? Does that transformation hinge upon the teacher's personality, level of intelligence, sense of humor, or other "mysterious something"? Or does that transformation instead depend upon the student's maturity level, commitment to learning, or interest in the subject matter? Over the years, many good teachers have touched my life, leaving a lasting imprint upon my mind and heart. However, only upon a few have I bestowed the honored title of "favorite." What makes the difference? Before you continue any further, take a few minutes to remember a favorite teacher and then make a mental list of the reasons why that teacher has earned such an honored place in your memory.

One of my favorite teachers was Dr. Ed Robinson, a professor of Christian education and now also dean of students at Nazarene Theological Seminary in Kansas City. Ed (as he invites his students to call him) was not only a favorite of mine but also a favorite of many. What made him so? Among other things, I remember a gentle spirit matched with strength of conviction, a genuine interest in students that exceeded the requirements of the syllabus, a confidence with which he gave us freedom to wander a bit in our pursuit of the truth, and a humility that invited us into an authentic learning partnership with him. Thankfully, my opportunities to know Ed extended beyond the walls of the classroom and into other settings like road trips, home visits, and the local church where we continue to serve together in ministry to youth. Ed was—and still is—a mentor, an anchor, a friend, and a favorite teacher.

The Story of God is all about a people's journey and a Guide who never stops calling them back home where they belong.

Who is your favorite teacher? Is it a kindergarten teacher who showed you a loving-kindness rooted in something deeper than your competency? A college English teacher who led you by example into a passion for critical thought and a pattern of lifelong learning? Or, is your favorite teacher one whose influence upon your life came through a somewhat less traditional role? A coach who never stopped believing in you, even when you were unsure if you believed in yourself? A pastor who responded to your telephone calls as if he had been hoping to hear from you rather than as if you were an interruption? A spouse whose faithful nurture of your soul you now recognize as a real means of God's grace? A parent who quietly but consistently modeled a healthy lifestyle for you that you now find yourself quietly modeling for your own children? In the end, whoever our favorite teachers are and wherever they have come from, all of them share at least this one thing in common: we want to be like them.

Sojourners and the Story

The Bible tells a timeless story of teaching and learning, of promise and fulfillment. In that epic narrative, sometimes God's guidance comes through overwhelming means like the parting of a sea, the fury of a prophet, or the blinding flash of angels appearing. But more often, God's guidance comes through quieter means like a whisper in the night, the blowing of a gentle wind, or a dove descending from heaven. The Story of God is all about a people's journey and a Guide who never stops calling them back home where they belong.

We who would teach are also guides. Our divinely appointed mission is to point others toward Christ and the Kingdom and to go with them on their journey. More clearly, our divine calling is first to follow Christ ourselves and then to invite others to come along with us on our journey. We take upon ourselves the weighty words of the apostle Paul when he writes, "Follow my example, as I follow the example of Christ" (1 Cor. 11:1). We agree in spirit and in practice with John the Baptist who spoke of Christ, "He must become greater; I must become less" (John 3:30). We learn how to guide others in the way of Christ, not by pointing to ourselves, but by pointing to Christ. In this manner, we all take part in the building up of the Church—the Body of Christ—as each member does its work (Eph. 4:16).

Teenagers need guides to show them the way of Christ in Scripture and in life. Many of today's teenagers may have learned to think about the Bible as something akin to a collection of fortune cookie proverbs strung end to end, meant to be cracked open and quickly scanned but often not very useful and certainly not very tasty. Teenagers need adult guides who can help them see for themselves the ever-fresh and ever-new direction that comes from the Word of the Lord. The stories of Scripture live as surely today as they did at their first telling and at their first living. Those stories are reborn in us as we weave their power and meaning into the fabric of our lives. They are reborn in us as we gain a new knowledge of the same God who also went with the children of Israel on their journey into the Promised Land. Teenagers need guides who know what it means to follow Christ through both history and direct experience.

Guidance means companionship on the journey. Teenagers do not need a compass or a map as much as they need a trustworthy friend to show them the way. Too often, we have tended to merely throw the map (the Bible) at them and say, "This book tells you how to get where you want to go. It tells you what to do. You are on your own now, and it is your responsibility to figure it out. I'll be praying for you, and have a nice trip."

Teenagers reject that style of leadership (if it is truly leadership at all). They will face much difficulty in learning to live out the Word of the Lord unless we are walking along with them on that journey. The Bible was never intended to be thrown at someone as a stand-alone book of helpful advice. Rather, the Bible is meant to be lived and breathed in the intersection of our daily lives together. That is why the Bible is full of stories about faith in the flesh instead of technical articles on theology or lists like "Seven Steps to Spiritual Success." As teenagers see us living out the faith in the details of our daily lives, they will want to walk alongside us. They know that our experience with the potholes, hazards, and detours on the road of life can help us help them walk through those difficult times. Our experience gives them reason for confidence and hope while they face the threatening crossroads of adolescence.

Teenagers struggle to find a faith that they can own with personal conviction, and our guiding presence plays an important role in that struggle. In the previous chapter, we discussed the formation of identity in teenage development. During adolescence, they rework their sense of self and their sense of meaning, moving from childhood toward adulthood. During this stage, the faith convictions they formed in childhood are poked and pushed in uncomfortable new ways. Their faith undergoes a time of critical reflection marked by hard questions and nagging doubts. In fact, they question not only their own faith but also the faith of their family and church. During this search for a deeper faith, teenagers need faithful leaders to nurture and affirm them along the way. This vital connection between youth and adults is the backbone of strong youth ministry and strong teaching.

Derrick's Story

Three doors down from my church, the identity and faith of a 16-year-old named Derrick are up for grabs. He lives with his mother, does not hear much at all from his father, and spends much of his time alone. All too often conflict and failure mark his days at school. Anger, confusion, fear, and despair hang over him like a cloud. The chaotic voices and images of hard-core rap music, MTV, and video games swirl around in his head. Several times a week, Derrick wanders into our office area, looking for someone to talk with, something to do, and something to believe.

The more we talk, the more I hear his false bravado giving way to the nagging questions that overwhelm his heart. "Where am I headed in life? Should I stay in school? What does my tomorrow look like? Do I matter to anyone? What is going to happen to me when I die? Would it really make any difference if I placed my trust in Christ?" As Derrick talks, I listen. Then, carefully, I begin to talk with him about a God who knew him and who loved him before he was ever born. A God who carefully designed Derrick to fit just right into a forever family called the king dom of God. A God who intends and very much desires to give Derrick a hope and a future full of love, purpose, joy, and peace. A God who has already said yes to Derric, and is now waiting and hoping for Derrick's yes in return. Those conversations usually get pretty quiet toward the end. The pauses lengthen. Eventually, we both end up sitting still and drinking in the peace and rest of the moment.

Derrick is on the way. He has not yet fully accepted the mercy and grace of Christ, but he is heading in that direction, slowly, surely. He sees light up ahead at the end of his darkness. He is incubating. The shell around him is beginning to break and new life is struggling within him to be born. And I am not recruiting him or selling him something. I am just God's messenger, a guide pointing the way to a God who will be no less faithful to Derrick than to me, and offering to walk with Derrick on a journey that we both can share. Although Derrick has not yet opened his life fully to the grace of God, something must be working right. *He keeps coming back for more.*

The Godbearing Life

This way of doing youth ministry is not new but is in fact a model thousands of years old, described quite vividly in Kenda Creasy Dean and Ron Foster's book *The Godbearing Life.* Drawing from the Annunciation narrative in Luke 1:26-38, they paint a picture of a God who calls and sends us, not by coercion but by courtship. First, a divinely appointed messenger comes to Mary, bringing words of God's affirmation:

"Good morning!
You're beautiful with God's beauty,
Beautiful inside and out!
God be with you" (Luke 1:28, TM).

Like Mary, we all want assurance within the deepest place of our selves—assurance that we are known and that we are loved. The angel continues, "Do not be afraid, Mary, you have found favor with God. You will be with child and give birth to a son, and you are to give him the name Jesus. He will be great and will be called the Son of the Most High. The Lord God will give him the throne of his father David, and he will reign over the house of Jacob forever; his kingdom will never end" (vv. 30-33).

Having announced God's divine yes to Mary, the angel now invites Mary to respond with her yes to God. Mary has received assurance of God's favor; now will she accept God's gracious invitation? At first, Mary is troubled. She is unsure. She questions; the angel gently persists. After a time of struggle, however, Mary ultimately embraces the call of God with an attitude of willing surrender: "'I am the Lord's servant,' Mary answered. 'May it be to me as you have said'" (v. 38). Dean and Foster summarize:

> From Mary's yes forward, she becomes "Godbearer," or as the Eastern Orthodox call her, *Theotokos*. Ministry does not end with Mary's transformation; it begins. . . . Youth ministry is a womb, an incubation ward for potential Godbearers as they struggle with the news that God is crazy in love with them, would die for them and, in fact, has. What youth need more than gung-ho adults are Godbearing adults, people whose own yes to God has transformed them into messengers of the gospel. Youth ministry does not just make Godbearers out of adults for youth; Godbearers convey God's affirmation and invitation to youth so that *they* become Godbearers, carrying Christ into the culture that adolescents inhale daily. The moment we say yes to God, we become bearers of God's work. From the second we lower our defenses—"Here am I, the servant of the Lord; let it be with me according to your word"—the Holy Spirit enters us, fills us, takes us over, changes everything about us, and, through us, the world in which we live *(1998).*

Is there any better picture of Christian teaching than this picture of the Godbearing life? Sometimes that teaching comes through time in Sunday School or Bible study, sometimes outside of the classroom. Sometimes that teaching comes through what is spoken, sometimes simply through what is shown. Whatever the setting, God calls us to nothing more, and to nothing less than this: that we, "who with unveiled faces all reflect the Lord's glory, are being transformed into his likeness with increasing glory" (2 Cor. 3:18) would share with teenagers God's invitation to enter into that lifelong journey alongside us.

Tensions Teachers Face

Teaching never comes without tension. Sometimes those conflicts and struggles are inward, sometimes outward, and sometimes both. For example, teaching at its very best brings to us feelings of deep satisfaction, intense joy, and genuine love. On the other hand, teaching at its worst assaults our souls with accusations of incompetence, restless thoughts, and feelings of resentment. Some days, teenagers surpass their ordinary selves, sparkling with enthusiasm, creativity, and vivid interest. On other days, they grumble and whine about boredom and frustration, transferring the responsibility for their unhappiness onto our shoulders. The teaching-learning encounter is a dynamic, ever-changing journey of invitation and response. The teacher plays a particularly critical role in guiding students through duty toward passion, away from superficiality into significance, and out of falsehood into truth.

To be honest, it is tempting to settle for superficiality and falsehood when we teach. The incessant teenage cry for entertainment and hype invites us to settle for proclaiming less than the whole truth. We sense how easy it could be to skate by on personality and easy answers when we realize that teenagers might let us get away with it. We know very well that, despite the ability of truth to encourage and uplift us, it sometimes quickly turns to rebuke us, embarrass us, and make us uncomfortable. Thus, we are tempted to declare as truth that which seems easy and safe instead of that which looks risky and difficult. Any wholehearted pursuit of the truth demands strength and courage from teachers and students alike.

> Any wholehearted pursuit of the truth demands strength and courage from teachers and students alike.

Authenticity vs. Role Playing

The first and most elemental tension all teachers face is that of authenticity vs. role playing. We struggle to know whether to reveal ourselves to our students, warts and all. We feel the burden of having to have it all together and so we wrestle with the temptation to role-play, to put up a facade of our real, flawed selves. We wonder if we should just stick to the lesson instead of getting off track or embarrassing ourselves by bringing our personal lives into the discussion. We would rather improve our class by finding a better teaching strategy or buying that elusive "right" curriculum instead of bringing our lessons to life by risking self-revelation. We sense that it would feel safer to control students with sarcasm or humorous patter than to let the silence of an unanswered question hang in the air. However, the best teaching does not begin with questions of "what," "how," or "why" but with "who." Parker Palmer, in his book *The Courage to Teach,* elaborates: "Good teaching cannot be reduced to technique; good teaching comes from the identity and integrity of the teacher. . . . As we learn more about who we are, we can learn techniques that reveal rather than conceal the personhood from which good teaching comes. . . . Authority comes as I reclaim my identity and integrity, remembering my self and my sense of vocation. Then teaching can come from the depths of my own truth—and the truth that is within my students has a chance to respond in kind" (1998).

Parker Palmer is saying that the best teaching is not a matter of technology but of personal authenticity. When we have not recognized God's work in our lives, we cannot teach it, no matter how skilled we may be. However, when we recognize and celebrate God's work within us, we cannot help but teach wherever we may go. We cannot help but get personal in the telling of God's Story, because the sweetest telling we know is that telling which is at work within us! The techniques we need to learn are not gimmicks or shortcuts. Rather, we need to gain proficiency in openly and honestly sharing with others our personal knowledge of God's mysterious and redeeming grace.

This is not to recommend that we view teaching teenagers as a therapeutic couch where we work out our own neuroses and hang-ups. On the contrary, our authority in teaching comes when we simply allow students to see what it means for us as growing Christians to "work out our salvation with fear and trembling" (Phil. 2:12). In the language of narrative theology, this is what entering the Story means. When we freely allow teenagers to walk with us on our journeys of struggle and hurt, joy and peace, then they are free to share their journeys with us also and our teaching gains real authority. Not an authority based upon "knowing it all" or upon coercive power, but an authority based upon authenticity, trust, and honesty.

Frederick Buechner, in his book *Telling Secrets,* offers several comments about authentic preaching that carry over by analogy to our concerns about authentic teaching: "[Preaching] is to proclaim a Mystery before which, before whom, even our most exalted ideas turn to straw. It is also to proclaim this Mystery with a passion that ideas alone have little to do with. It is to try to put the Gospel into words not the way you would compose an essay but the way you would write a poem or a love letter — putting your heart into it, your own excitement, most of all your own life. It is to speak words that you hope may, by grace, be bearers not simply of new understanding but of new life both for the ones you are speaking to and also for you" (1991).

As you think about your teaching just now, what do you notice? Do you notice self-protection or self-disclosure? Do you see a tendency toward perfectionism and authoritarianism, or do you recognize a humility that is free to confess both personal victories and personal struggles? Does your teaching often feel like an opportunity for negative self-criticism and even condemnation, or does it feel more like a breath of fresh air and a means of grace for you and for others? Does your teaching come from that place in your heart where love letters are composed, or does it come instead from a place in your mind that reads like a technical manual? Authenticity is dangerous and risky, but so is the journey of grace. Dare to move beyond role-playing. Dare to be real.

Faith vs. Doubt

The second tension that teachers encounter is that of faith vs. doubt. I remember my first Wednesday night leading a youth service, and a little later, my first altar call. Regretfully, after both experiences I felt the same emotions: nervousness, fear, and doubt. Nervous because I lacked the peace and assurance that I had performed well. Fear because I imagined that the teenagers might have sensed my nervousness. Doubt because I did not fully believe in myself, my teenagers, or most importantly, in the God who had called me to pastor them. Now I can see that in those moments, my confidence had been placed, not in the power of the gospel and in the God behind it, but in the messenger (myself) and in the recipients (the youth group). Consequently, the burden of performance became unbearable and the tension of doubt overshadowed my faith.

The same thing holds true for parenting. How often do we find ourselves looking at our children with eyes of discouragement and disbelief as, once again, they do the very thing we've told them a hundred times not to do? "How long, O Lord, how long?" we cry. In those times, the codependent impulse to manipulate, coerce, and control colors our whole perception. In frustration, we imagine that "this kid's never going to get it unless I do something about it right *now*!" So, we launch into the routine of pushing, prodding, guilting, and motivating our children toward the behavior we feel is long overdue. In such moments, we forget that God will be just as faithful to guide our children into mature faith as He was with us. In such moments, we suffer the burden of trying to engineer another person's growth according to our personal timetables instead of faithfully trusting in God's time and in God's way. In such moments, doubt in the other person and doubt in God overshadows the confidence of faith.

Our failure to hold on to faith instead of grasping for control and coercion has been popularly referred to as practical atheism. Practical atheism is a Christian heresy in which a person professes faith in God's redemptive grace, but then acts as if redemption was his or her own work instead of God's work. Do you know any practical atheists? Have you ever believed or behaved like one? We run the risk of turning to practical atheism when we mistakenly assume that God needs us to manage everyone else for Him (if only these teenagers would just listen to us!). Flattering ourselves, our imaginations tell us that we are little messiahs who hold the keys to fixing the problems of other people. The trouble with that attitude is this: in such moments, we have forgotten that there is only one Lord, and that we are not He! Thus, we end up frustrated with others who fail to live up to our subjective standards of spiritual growth, doubting their integrity. We end up frustrated with ourselves, doubting our ability to teach effectively (if we taught better, wouldn't people straighten up?). We even end up frustrated with God, doubting that He is really "blessing" our ministry. Overwhelmed with faithless frustration, little messiahs burn out very quickly.

Linda J. Vogel describes the faith of a teacher in her book *Teaching and Learning in Communities of Faith:* "Because we know and at the same time know that we do not know all, there is a freedom to be vulnerable, to trust that God is at work in the process as well as in the faith story, and to claim the promise that God's grace is sufficient. We are freed from the burden that we are somehow responsible for the decisions of those we teach. We can admit that we do not have all the answers" (1991).

When we remember that God "is able to do immeasurably more than all we ask or imagine, according to *his* power that is at work within us," then we gain faith to teach (Eph. 3:20, emphasis added). When we remember that adults and teenagers alike are partners in the gospel and that God is redeeming us all, then we may faithfully declare to teenagers that "he who began a good work in you will carry it on to completion until the day of Christ Jesus" (Phil. 1:6). When we look at our teenagers, remembering that "it is God who works in [them] to will and to act according to his good purpose" (Phil. 2:13), then we have every reason to believe in the Lordship of Christ. Jesus is Teacher; Jesus is Healer. Jesus is Lord; we are not.

As you think about your teaching, what do you notice? How often do you doubt yourself or your performance because you are not seeing the results that you want to see? Do you ever get angry with the teenagers that you teach because they are not responding with the faith that you expect to see? Are you looking for the exit door of ministry because you don't feel like you can handle any more of the tension between your expectations and the failure of others to meet them? Let that doubt go and remember that you have every reason for faith. The Spirit of Christ is still writing new chapters in the Story of God. While it is true that you play a critical role in the telling of those stories, remember that their telling does not depend upon you as much as it depends upon God.

Connection vs. Isolation

Another tension confronting teachers is that of connection vs. isolation. Isolation is the deadly enemy of a church that needs connection in order to live. The tyranny of technology increasingly threatens our connection to one another. Our teenagers know the mind-numbing reality of spending countless hours alone with the Internet, with a video game, with headphones, lost in their own self-absorbed worlds. When they gather socially, their default activity is often video rental or moviegoing, a passive group activity that ends up stifling creative conversation by focusing all eyes upon the screen images instead of upon one another. Technology has significantly added to the social and emotional inertia that characterizes so many teenagers. They are not used to thinking critically or reflectively about themselves. Teenagers who are not used to telling their stories from Monday to Saturday will need help and encouragement to do so on Sunday.

Teachers who share their personal stories with teenagers will create an environment of safety in which teenagers can also share their personal stories with each other. As we discussed earlier, the teacher's task is to lead the way in self-disclosure. Sharing relevant life experience happens easiest and best when the teacher has lived as a learner with the text all week long, instead of approaching it as a user in an hour's preparation time. By talking about the text's claim on their own lives, teachers make it safe for others to do the same. When sharing your story, remember to connect it with the text under consideration. You may want to avoid sharing some particulars if doing so would distract your students from God's action in the story. For example, it is often not necessary to give real names, particularly if doing so would negatively affect the person named. Remind your students that all stories should remain confidential within the class unless other permission is given. Do not allow cutdowns or ridicule in response to any story. Assure them that it is acceptable if the story does not have a happy ending or concrete resolution. The intersection of faith and life is messy and tangled, not neat and tidy. Most importantly, encourage your students to always ask and answer the question "Where was God in that part of my story, and what was He doing there?" A bigger question they may learn to ask is "Where am I in God's Story, and what am I doing there?"

In order for you and your students to enjoy a vital connection, it is also necessary to spend significant time with one another. We need to earn the right to be heard. That does not necessarily come through quantity, but certainly through quality of time spent together. Teaching Sunday School involves more than an hour on Sunday morning. In order for connection to occur, we need to cultivate spiritual friendships with teenagers in which we allow them to see faith enfleshed within the details of our personal lives. Faith that is preached at teenagers instead of faith lived before them will most often fail to touch their lives. Francis of Assisi is credited with these words: "Preach the gospel at all times, and if necessary, use words." For teachers, these words ring equally true. Certainly it would be easier to just show up for Sunday School, talk about Jesus for an hour, and then disappear until the next Sunday. However, your witness on Sunday is more powerful when teenagers see it in action outside of the classroom.

As you think about your teaching, what do you notice? Do you live with the text most of the week so that the Story of God can have enough time to intersect with your own story? Do you live with your teenagers during the week in order to identify where the Story of God intersects their stories? When you and your teenagers discuss the text, does the conversation always stay safely objective, or do things ever get personal? Are you willing to discuss your spiritual brokenness and struggles as well as your victories? Are you doing most of the talking on Sunday morning, or are teenagers talking too? When one of them does dare to speak, in what ways do you or anyone else offer appreciation and assurance? As their teacher, create a safe space where teenagers can securely risk telling each other the truth about their own lives.

Security vs. Superficiality

Eventually, every teacher faces the tension of security vs. superficiality. Jesus faced this same tension in the wilderness after John baptized Him and before He began His earthly ministry (Matt. 4:1-11). In the book *In the Name of Jesus,* Henri Nouwen vividly describes both Jesus' struggle and the related tensions that all Christian leaders face (1993). In the wilderness, Satan comes to Jesus with three "Let's Make a Deal"-type propositions. Again and again, Satan invites Jesus to forfeit His messianic integrity in exchange for immediate and superficial gratification. Nouwen refers to the first temptation as the temptation of relevancy. Here, Satan tempts Jesus to validate himself by doing something useful and relevant, something that people really "need"—turning stones into bread to satisfy their hunger. The second temptation is the temptation of popularity. Here, Satan tempts Jesus to do something spectacular and impressive, something that people will stand up and cheer for—throwing himself down from the Temple peak to be rescued by angels. The last temptation is the temptation of power. Here, Satan offers Jesus the loyalty and allegiances of the world's kingdoms—if Jesus will only bow down and worship Satan. In all three temptations, Satan tempts Jesus to give away the security of His God-given identity in exchange for the quick and easy road to immediate gratification.

In our pursuit of security—a worthwhile and healthy pursuit in and of itself—we sometimes settle for superficial means of gaining that security. When we teach, we risk ourselves in a very public way and hope that those whom we teach will accept us. However, in those times when we feel rejected, humiliation and depression can crush our spirits. Carelessly, we may base our security and identity upon the reactions of others toward us, rather than upon the calling and the grace of God to teach. In those moments of carelessness, we may find ourselves pandering to students and diluting the integrity of our teaching merely to gain good standing among them. At our worst, we become like Esau, abandoning the security of our God-given identity in exchange for the superficial pottage of pleasing people and gaining popularity. It takes a teacher with a strong sense of self and an unswerving loyalty to God's eternal truth to withstand the public pressure to be a people pleaser.

In practical terms, what does it mean to choose security over superficiality? Simply, it means that we cannot allow the approval of our teenagers to displace God's approval as the measuring stick by which we evaluate our performance. Instead, we must remember to ask ourselves the question first asked by the apostle Paul, "Am I now trying to win the approval of men, or of God? Or am I trying to please men? If I were still trying to please men, I would not be a servant of Christ" (Gal. 1:10). All of us want to be liked, but that cannot become our end or goal in teaching. We cannot hold back from challenging students' assumptions and prejudices out of a fear of rejection. There is a time to push and, in fact, a time to ease up in the teaching experience, but that time must be based upon the readiness level of our teenagers, not upon our personal insecurity. Henri Nouwen concludes: "But when we are securely rooted in personal intimacy with the source of life, it will be possible to remain flexible without being relativistic, convinced without being rigid, willing to confront without being offensive, gentle and forgiving without being soft, and true witnesses without being manipulative" (1993).

What are those things that firmly anchor us to the source of life instead of the shifting sands of others' approval? To begin with, we need a prayerful spirit. We need a heart that quietly and patiently listens for the voice of God saying, "I am your Father. I am your strength. I value you. I am your peace. I have gifted you, yet I will use you in your weakness. Rest in My presence, and let Me teach through you." Also, we need spiritual friendships in our lives that move beyond the teenagers we teach. We need truthful relationships with others who will know when to comfort or challenge us, when to hear our confession or call us to repentance. Finally, we need to cultivate the spiritual practice of discernment. Discernment is that habit by which we intentionally and carefully sift through our own assumptions in fulfillment of the apostle Paul's admonition to "test everything. Hold on to the good. Avoid every kind of evil" (1 Thess. 5:21-22). A prayerful heart, honest friendships, and the practice of spiritual discernment are the three things that keep us securely connected to God's approval instead of the approval of others.

As you think about your teaching, what do you notice? Do you evaluate the success of your teaching based upon what is seen or what is unseen? Do you ever find yourself acting or speaking in ways that have much more to do with bolstering your sense of self rather than with proclaiming the gospel of Christ? How often do you take time to stop and listen for the still, small voice of God assuring you that He is well-pleased with you? Do you have any mature spiritual friendships that are marked by a mutual freedom to share both grace and truth with one another? Are you cultivating an attitude of reflection and discernment? The words of that old gospel hymn are true: "On Christ the solid rock I stand; / all other ground is sinking sand." God and God alone can give us the security that we need to teach.

Staying True to the Story

We teach the Story of God, with the historical narrative of Scripture as our starting point, but with the ongoing narratives of our lives in the Kingdom as the new context. The Father still calls out to His creation; the Savior still redeems the lost; the Spirit still guides the Church. God acts, and we respond; the Story goes on. Teenagers, in their search for a self and for belonging,

> Teenagers, in their search for a self and for belonging, long for a story that can describe and direct their lives.

long for a story that can describe and direct their lives. We who teach know that they may most perfectly find that which they seek in the eternal Story of God. We want to help teenagers recognize and confess that God already has chosen them to play a critical part in His Story. Our teaching is like detective work in which we search the past for clues that God has been at work there, in order that we may find guidance and know hope for the future.

As we teach the story of God, we must let it inform not only the content of our teaching but also the attitudes with which we teach. To teach God's Story is first to live it with openness, honesty, and courage before our teenagers; this is *authenticity*. To teach God's Story is to confess our *faith* in God's unfailing grace that works in teenagers and teachers alike "to will and to act according to his good purpose" (Phil. 3:13). To teach God's Story is to appreciate our partnership in the adventure of faith and to deepen our *connection* with one another. To teach God's Story is to rest in the *security* that comes from allowing God to be the source of our esteem before all others.

Frederick Buechner, in his book *Now and Then,* explained that if he had to sum up the essence of everything he had to say as a novelist and a preacher, it would be something like this: "Listen to your life. See it for the fathomless mystery that it is. In the boredom and pain of it no less than in the excitement and gladness: touch, taste, smell your way to the holy and hidden heart of it because in the last analysis all moments are key moments, and life itself is grace" (1983). May these words comfort and guide us as we seek to fully live and to faithfully teach the ongoing Story of God.

CHAPTER 5

NARRATIVE

TEACHING:

LEARNING HOW

TO TEACH

THE STORY

OF GOD

DEAN BLEVINS

When teachers learn narrative teaching they are surprised by the results. Students not only learn the Bible lesson but also are changed by it! Our responsibility as youth workers is to learn the best way to teach our students. The narrative method is one of the most faithful and effective approaches to teaching. Narrative teaching requires some advance knowledge and planning if we are going to be good teachers. We can be sidetracked by a number of misconceptions. Once we get the big picture, however, narrative teaching can become almost second nature. It is crucial that we learn to teach in such a way that we respect God's Story. In this chapter we will learn about the common pitfalls, the basic structure of narrative teaching, the main steps, and finally some important tools to make our teaching both effective and faithful.

The Promise and the Problems

When Christian teachers come to the realization that the narrative method is a powerful approach to transformation in the postmodern world, they naturally respond with a desire to use it in their ministry. Now that we *know* narrative is important, we want to *do* something with it so that we can *become* faithful narrative teachers and preachers. To intersect our students' life stories with God's Story gives us a fresh vision for our ministry. We feel we can really make a difference for the sake of our students and for the sake of God's kingdom.

We also risk falling flat on our faces. This is particularly true if we are not aware of the problems associated with a poor understanding of narrative method.

The first real danger of narrative method is to assume that teaching is just telling stories, particularly stories with a specific moral ending. Too often we either try to force the moral principle into a biblical story or else we invent a story to support our claims. A common example of a poorly told and poorly timed story comes out of certain evangelism strategies with children and youth. Often the stories are fictional and describe children (little Johnny or Susie) who are both disobedient to their parents and will not listen to God. One day little Johnny or Susie acts very badly and ignores God. On leaving the house Johnny or Susie disobeys his or her parents and runs out onto the road, only to be struck by a truck! The "moral" quickly becomes that children should obey God (and their parents) or terrible things might happen to them. A youthful version of this has teenagers getting wrapped up in drugs or some other form of degradation to the point they are killed or commit suicide (an alternative demise to the truck). In each setting the stories (often more fictional than real) are only window dressings to a thinly disguised moral warning that God will get you if you don't obey. This approach inevitably places God in a scary light (the eternal truck driver looking to flatten willful but unsuspecting children). These stories also provide the wrong motivation for coming to Jesus, since our running from evil has more to do with individual *personal* fear than godly love.

If we do not create bad stories in fear, we often trivialize them through humor. "Did you hear the story of the kid with the bad complexion . . . ?" Jokes are often used to gain the trust of a group at the beginning of a session. Caution, however, should prevail when punctuating a moral principle with humor. The problem with humor is that the stories often make fun of youth (or adults) without really connecting to the biblical principle.

Some stories are effective. Usually they find their theme in the everyday life and struggles of people (much like Jesus' parables) with surprising results. Often the story does not have to close with a "moral" since the story itself reveals truth in its telling. (Rule of thumb: if you constantly have to explain the moral of the story, then you probably do not need to tell the story.) Here is an example of a story that reveals grace more than supporting a moral:

Jenny (not her real name) was worried. In a moment of passion and poor choices, she had made a sophomore decision that would lead to a lifetime of consequences. During pregnancy she had decided to keep the child rather than abort. Now the family was three, her divorced mom, herself, and the baby. Her worry was about the small country church they attended. What would the people think? They had been supportive financially, and several individuals had stepped up to help with the child, but what did they <u>think</u> of this young girl's decision to try to make the best of her mistake? When Jenny arrived at church she had forgotten it was Mother's Day. This revelation only added to the anxiety by making her painfully aware of her own failure as a daughter.

The church had a ritual for each Mother's Day. At the beginning of worship, a contest was held for mothers. The prizes were single red roses. The pastor called for the mother with the most children as well as the mother with the most family attending the worship service. (Normally the second award was given to the mother who had the most "influence" in coercing her children to show up on time.) There was an award to the mother with the longest church membership as well as to the oldest living mother. Finally, there came the awards for the newest mother and the youngest mother in the congregation. Jenny was surprised to hear her name. Reluctantly she rose to go forward. The congregation began to applaud as she saw and received the two roses. It dawned on her that there was a good chance that while she might not always be the newest mother in this church, she might well be the youngest mother for quite a while. Jenny realized that every year, at Mother's Day, she would probably hear the loving applause of that congregation. And every year, for many years, she heard just that.

If we try to turn everything in our lives into a biblical allegory or some fictional Aesop's fable, we often end up with a cartoon account of everyday life that has no real relevance. Like a sermon made up strictly of illustrations, our teaching offers very little content to connect story and life. Telling stories is nice, but what are we trying to say about God's Story in a systematic way? Storytelling is a form of narrative that can be powerful when used carefully, but it may not be the best way to teach consistently in formal sessions to make sure people understand the whole Story of God.

When we teach God's Story we have to trust it.

Storytelling is actually one of two great dangers in narrative teaching. The other danger is that we will try to control the moral of the story through our teaching. We get so focused on the final point of the lesson that we find ourselves once again delivering dry information rather than authentic narrative teaching. We turn the greatest Story ever told into a computer manual. When we teach God's Story we have to trust it; we should not invent fake stories to make sure everyone gets the "punch line."

Narrative is messy (much like our lives are messy) and often unpredictable (much like God's grace is unpredictable) so we cannot always guarantee the outcome of the lesson. What makes narrative such a messy approach is that we are often asking our students certain questions about their lives that might create unpredictable responses. When we try to get at new issues or challenge the assumptions of how we live, we invite our students and ourselves to look at the world in an entirely new light. The same is true when we go to Scripture asking entirely new questions of familiar passages. Frankly, we cannot anticipate all the answers we might receive from our students' lives, from the Bible, or even from our own perspective. We often get a brand-new insight into what our lives should be, and it isn't always easy to blend these new ideas into our old ways of living. In truth, struggling to make sense of new but unanticipated knowledge is the best part of narrative teaching. We relinquish control of the outcome of the lesson so that we are surprised by what God might do through the scripture or through our lives. We may end up learning as much as our students, which is a good but scary thought. Ultimately we have to learn to trust the Holy Spirit and try to be faithful to God's leading.

So if narrative teaching is neither indiscriminant storytelling nor rigid, tightly controlled lesson plans, what is it? Can we be open to God's leading and yet employ a consistent method in order to be faithful in our teaching? How do we utilize the best teaching methods that are also true to a narrative understanding of teaching and learning? Can we teach in such a way that respects the Story of God while modeling our learning around human and biblical narratives?

We can accomplish narrative teaching if we adopt an approach that includes stories and life experiences. Our teaching not only resembles telling a good story but also allows people to explore their personal and community stories (both the good and the bad) in intersection with God's ongoing Story.

Two Clues to Narrative Teaching

Any narrative teaching begins by understanding the nature of a good story. Storytelling is an art, but normally each story follows a regular pattern. The scene is set (providing both location and characters in the story), a tension occurs (either through anticipation or conflict), followed by a climax, often with a moment of surprise. In the final stage the story seeks to provide a resolution, tying up loose ends to what has happened, pointing to a new future, living happily ever after. We use this pattern both in simple stories and elaborate dramas. For instance, two students meet for lunch:

"Where did you go last week?"

"I went on vacation out west." (The scene is set.)

"Was it a good trip?"

"Oh wow, it was a great trip, you wouldn't believe what I saw!"

"Yeah, tell me about it" (The tension to know.)

"I saw the Grand Canyon and, dude, it was unreal, the size of that place!" (Climax.)

"Really? You going back someday?"

"Yeah, I can't wait to go back for a full week and really explore the place." (Resolution.)

Even simple lunch conversations have a narrative form if we want to make the conversation interesting. We often repeat stories because we have found something truly unique in the telling that is both interesting and exciting. Action-adventure movies follow the same pattern, where the conflict builds to a climactic confrontation between good and evil. Most of the time we know who will win (the stars of the movie), but *how* they will win is crucial. The "how" surprises us (if it is a decent story) even if the rest of the story is pretty predictable. Stories build toward a climax, a surprise that often changes the nature of the story from beginning to end.

If narrative teaching is going to be effective, it needs to set the stage, have a plot with some tension, include a climax (a surprising turn of events), and provide students with an opportunity to see how that climax resolves the whole lesson. When we learn to take time to *build* toward a climax—a moment of new awareness based on God—and then help our students make sense of this new perspective, we are getting close to our job as teachers.

But good teaching needs more. Almost every popular approach to Bible teaching has to come to terms with time. Time locates where we begin and end our story. Most education theorists agree that the best teaching method begins with the students' current experience. We begin in the present where the students live. Once we have connected with the students on their ground, we can then turn to the content we want to teach. For Bible teachers this means we turn to the past, the time of the Bible. The third step is to then return to the present, to make some connection with the scripture (as shaped and interpreted in the past) and the students' present lives. Often understood as the application phase in teaching, this stage includes not only what we should do in the present but what we will also do in the future. By the end of the lesson we have actually used every aspect of time: past, present, and future. We begin in the present (to connect with the students), move to the past (to understand the Bible), return to the present (to connect the Bible to life), and finally focus on the future to see how what we have learned will change us.

68

All good Bible teachers know that the Bible bridges personal experience with timely Bible teaching: as narrative teachers we first explore issues in our **present lives** (and the problems associated with them). We then return to the **past** to learn all we can from the Story of God, bringing our understanding of the past into a conversation with our **present** lives and then work toward a *future* changed by our new understanding. Good narrative teaching combines the best of the structure of storytelling and timely Bible teaching. Once these approaches are combined, we can move into a comprehensive approach to narrative teaching.

A Comprehensive Method of Narrative Teaching[1]

Narrative teaching takes three broad themes and converts them into six basic steps to teach the Story of God. The three themes can be understood as three basic questions.

1. *What's wrong with this picture?* (Describing and critiquing everyday **life**)
2. *How does God surprise us?* (Entering into the biblical story expecting a new answer from God's **truth**)
3. *Now what?* (Deciding how to go forward with a **vision** of what we have celebrated and learned)

The first question begins in the present where students live. The question also sets the stage and raises the tension of the lesson. Students are allowed to describe their present lives, but we also want to explore how their current situation is a problem (either by what is missing or through the conflict they often experience).

The second question not only returns us to the past but also helps us listen to the Story of God for a new way of thinking and acting. We are seeking a climax to the tension, some way that the scripture unexpectedly changes our assumptions of how the world works. Frankly, we probably know the final outcome of the story (since most of us have read the end of the Book). What we are looking for are those surprising insights that reveal something more of what God thinks and how God acts! It is one thing to say you can go to heaven, but it is quite another to realize that it is only by grace through faith that you get there! So God surprises us through His Story even with the most familiar questions. Finally, we have to resolve what we are going to do with this new information (if it is truly new). That includes celebrating or living in awe of this new knowledge we have received from God. Our response includes not only our past but also our future, particularly since God's Story is also about the future.

Six Steps for Solid Teaching

Once we have the three basic themes down, we can elaborate on the themes by breaking them up into separate steps for easier planning. Here are six detailed steps under the headings of LIFE, TRUTH, and VISION that lead you toward being an accomplished narrative teacher (Hampton and Edwards 1999).[2] The steps are designed to be used in a 45 minute to one-hour teaching session.

Life

Start the lesson with two steps designed to introduce the topic, and then help students thoughtfully reflect on ways the topic relates to their lives. Introduce the LIFE theme of the lesson creatively, but do not rely on gimmicks or artificial activities to merely grab students' attention. Use activities that get students to describe and evaluate their real-life experiences and behaviors. You can then lead students to consider what these experiences and actions mean. The LIFE phase of the lesson should start from where the students are in relation to the topic and then carefully lead them to consider the topic at deeper levels of meaning. You can use the right activities to accomplish two essential parts of life by following the following guidelines.

Step one: Use activities that lead the students to describe what they have experienced or how they behave, relative to the lesson topic. Help students recall, reenact, or otherwise describe their real-life experiences or behaviors. Students should *describe* their world and their place in it (concrete actions and events), rather than discuss ideas or present their views on an issue (abstract concepts). For example, in a lesson on prayer, ask students to describe what they say or what they have heard other people say when praying (concrete action).[3] This approach is much better than asking them to define prayer (an abstract concept) since it names a direct action.

Older students will probably have more life experience from which to draw, so they can describe how they live and act (for instance, what they have experienced as a result of their prayers). The activities you create should aim at helping these older students remember or reenact what they did, how they felt, and so forth. Younger students have less life experience and may need to have their experience built into the lesson. You can create experiences directly (have them pray for one another) or though in-class simulation (have them role-play how other people pray). You can also introduce experience by having students observe or read case studies that deal with the topic (including reading printed prayers from the Bible or from great devotional writers). Any opening activity should take about 5 to 8 minutes in class.

Step two: The second step includes activities that probe deeper into the experiences and issues described in the first step. Here the task is to lead students to discover *why* they act the way they do and what the results would be, even if the students do not actually engage in the activity. (In other words asking, "What is the problem?") Several strategies can accomplish this. You can help the students uncover the motives or assumptions behind their actions: Why do they act in a certain way? They can also project the likely consequences of their actions if they were to continue: What will happen as a result of their actions? If the topic relates to certain beliefs or doctrines, have the students look for possible logical outcomes: What is the logical conclusion of this or that belief? Students should confront the question of whether their actions are likely to produce the result they would like or hope for.

You need to know that this process may involve exploring certain dead ends. Sometimes the students will offer motives that may not adequately explain why people behave the way they do. You may need to stay with the questions a little longer since ongoing exploration will probably reveal deeper motives, or additional past experiences may provide better explanations. Students may discover that the likely consequences of their actions may not be compatible with their hopes and dreams or may not be consistent with who they hope to be.

Take the topic of prayer as an example. Some students may think initially that their unanswered prayers are a result of a lack of faith on their part or incorrect technique. Further discussion or questioning may reveal these answers to be inadequate or incorrect explanations and thus, a dead end. The real problem might be in their definition of what prayer is or who God is. Allow time and opportunity for students to reach these dead ends.

One of the best devices to accomplish the goals of this second step is to create good discussion questions that get students to think about what they are doing or believing. Above all, get students thinking and talking about real life-experiences. Make sure to do sound research for true-to-life teen views and dilemmas. Be sure that you allow a little more time for this step than you did for introducing the experiences and behaviors since asking in-depth questions takes time. Allowing 10 to 12 minutes should provide the right amount of time for this second step of the LIFE phase of the lesson.

The students will realize that the Bible, God's Story, not only informs their life but also transforms it.

One reminder: community building, which serves to establish (or reestablish) connections between students, is also an important part of any lesson. While community building can occur at any point in the lesson, it most frequently appears in LIFE. The community building approach can include a review of the previous lesson or can simply include the students' descriptions of their lives as they begin relating to the topic and sharing with each other. Following the steps described above helps build community, but you should always review your work to make sure that there are opportunities for the students to interact together.

Truth

The second major movement of the lesson presents or explores God's often-surprising perspective on the lesson topic. It also leads students to relate their experience with God's perspective primarily from "inside" the Bible. Instead of trying to relate the Bible to our lives (where our experiences are the most important), we are trying our best to hear what the Bible has to say so that we are relating our lives to the Bible, to God's Story! Just like the LIFE phase, there are two steps to this process.

Step one: First, students discover God's perspective as they explore the Christian Story, with the teacher acting as the one who passes on the Story to the next generation. You are encouraged to present this information in terms of story—that is, using elements of character, setting, plot, action, conflict, resolution, and so forth.

You should tell students (or help them discover) answers to questions like the following: Who are the characters and what issues were they dealing with? What was their relationship to God and what role did they have in the story of God's people? You should use storytelling and lecture methods on occasion, but not in every lesson. Use a variety of methods to explore the Christian Story, remembering to bring out the elements associated with stories.

Many sources may be used to tell the Christian Story, such as the biographies of historical or contemporary Christians, resources from Church history, and good contemporary scholarship. However, the prime source material is the Bible, specifically the passage(s) that are central to your lesson. Good curriculum will include some basic information, but you can do further research on your own.

You can use three basic components of Bible study to develop your lesson. Every lesson should focus on the third component, but many lessons will need to address the first two in order to help students understand the message and how it ties in to the overarching themes of the biblical story. (Always assume that many, if not most, students know less about the Bible than we anticipate.) For the **ABC** approach to unlocking a scripture passage, follow these steps:

A. Identify the author, date, historical and cultural background, as well as the primary reason for writing the passage and any significant words in the passage.

B. Look for the type of literature that describes your Bible passage (narrative, poetry, gospel, letter, apocalyptic, etc.). You should try to identify the literary devices used in the passage (metaphor, parable, irony, foreshadowing, hyperbole, etc.). Look also for the relation of the passage to the overall message of the book and the Bible.

C. Check how people have interpreted and applied the passage throughout history. What doctrines have been shaped by it? What actions have Christians taken in response to it? How has the passage been used in worship and the Christian calendar?

This ABC approach should give you a good background for understanding the biblical passage(s) you are studying. Often a good study Bible, your curriculum resource materials, or a single volume commentary/dictionary will provide much of this information.

Step two: The second major step of the TRUTH movement is to encourage students to compare the Christian Story to their experience. In doing so, they may experience the dawning of a new realization or change of perspective. This often comes as a surprise that either confirms or challenges their commonly accepted behavior and beliefs. Sometimes the Bible turns their assumptions upside down by suggesting a whole new perspective on their problems. Students may respond in one or more of the following ways:

A. The Christian Story may reveal a problem in our students' present action. A student sees that the Christian Story contradicts the way he or she is living, or it highlights the problems the student already senses in his or her life (perhaps first revealed in the LIFE phase of the lesson).

B. The Christian Story affirms current students' behavior and beliefs, providing assurance and encouragement that they are headed in the right direction. Another similar response is that the Christian Story sheds light on students' struggles or doubts and thus helps to resolve a dilemma (again, perhaps first revealed in the LIFE phase of the lesson).

C. The Christian Story may lead students to create new ways of living that include the truths of the Christian Story but also adds to and enriches the continuing Christian Story. A student might find a new way to show God's love (for instance through compassionate activities) that actually enriches the whole youth group and starts a new chapter in the life of a church.

Regardless of the type of response, the students will realize that the Bible, God's Story, not only informs their life but also transforms it. When the Christian Story is taught, the whole person is challenged.

To avoid sending the message that the TRUTH phase is strictly "head work," vary the learning activities with active movement, visual, and audio learning aids/methods. (Chapter 6 contains more information on how to do this.) You can use some discussion questions that call for a recital of the facts, to make sure students understand the facts and meaning, but don't stop there. Ask questions that invite students to respond with personal answers, not just what they think the teacher wants to hear. For example, not "What is prayer?" but "How do you understand prayer?" or "What could our understanding of prayer mean for your life?" Both of the steps in the TRUTH section can be combined in 15 to 20 minutes. Once students have a good sense of the message of the Bible passage, they are ready to move forward, back into their own lives and in to the future.

Vision

The third and last major movement of the lesson should help students celebrate their new insights into what it means to be God's people and then move them toward becoming an active participant in the Christian Story. As with the first two movements of the lesson, VISION also has two steps.

Step one: Usually, the first step of the VISION phase of the lesson should focus on celebrating the good news of the Christian Story as discovered in the TRUTH phase. The dominant tone should be one of play, relief, and praise as a natural response. You can guide students to use their creativity to express themselves in new or traditional expressions of faith. These expressions can be songs, hymns, Scripture readings or paraphrases, creeds, dramas, liturgical formulas, banners, art or writing projects that highlight key phrases or concepts from the lesson. Remember to help students celebrate not only the facts and stories they have learned but also their new identities through being or becoming a member of God's people.

The second step of the VISION phase should aim to help students live their lives in new ways, based upon their discovery of who God is, what He has done, and who they can be because of Him. They should be given opportunities to make decisions that commit them to joining or remaining a part of God's Story. They may be asked to decide what role or character they will fulfill in God's Story. This call to participate should be specific enough that students can act on their decisions. Although students may be given help to do this, the lesson should not simply give students tools to cope with life; rather, they should be given a new identity from which to view and respond to life.

Although the other steps of the lesson follow a strict sequence, you can reverse the order of the VISION steps as described above, with the acts of celebration appearing last. Avoid using too many commitment cards, contracts, covenants, and so forth. Savvy students will quickly tire of weekly commitments that are on paper only. Provide opportunities for them to act on what they have learned and decided. Take care not to manipulate or coerce decisions from students. Instead, offer them an invitation to join God's Story. However, indicate clearly what is involved in such decisions and which decisions will lead one to stand outside of God's Story. The activities for both TRUTH steps combined should be 10 to 15 minutes.

Putting it all together takes some time, but you end up with a great lesson that respects the students and the gospel at the same time. Once you have the basic structure down, you will be able to teach students so that they connect to God's Story in a brand-new way. The six steps keep your lesson on track, helping you to really understand the strengths and limitations of our current lives. The steps then carry you through the Christian Story (the Bible) carefully, helping you to be alert to what God has to offer. Finally the steps give your students plenty of opportunities to celebrate and apply what they have learned. Once you have the basics down, you can enhance your teaching by employing some additional skills.

Basic Tools for Narrative Teaching

Even with a thorough knowledge of the six steps, you will need to learn some important skills for yourself as a teacher and learner as well as for your students and colearners. These skills help us in preparing the lesson and our classrooms, in teaching the lesson and in understanding how students are changed through our efforts. Each of these tools will go a long way in increasing your effectiveness and faithfulness as a teacher.

1. Devote time to preparing the lesson in advance and live the scripture throughout the week. I have found that the number one key to any good lesson is to read the lesson early (preferably on the Sunday afternoon following the last lesson) and read the scripture from the lesson daily. Frankly, you cannot teach the story unless you have walked around inside it yourself. Most educators who have studied creativity know that our best ideas come from an early familiarity with the lesson. When we are comfortable with the scripture and focus of the story, new ideas will almost literally pop

up each day. We will have more than we need to teach our lesson.

2. If you want students to look at their lives and say, "What's wrong with this picture?" you need to *ask the right questions.* Remember that there is more than one type of question and the type often opens or limits student discussion. Factual questions normally have only one right answer and may help get a discussion back on track ("What does the Bible say about our topic?") but often limit discussion by suggesting one right answer. Value questions ("What is your opinion?") can also limit discussion since students often have a personal investment in the answer. Analytical questions ("*How* does the passage address this issue?") and productive (brainstorming) questions actually encourage a lot more input.

   Remember also that questions can imply three different audiences: general, community, and personal. Remember that the more personal a question is, the more threatening it can be. I often begin classes with general, productive questions and gradually work through community analytical and factual questions to end up with personal value questions at the end of the lesson. Consider the sticky subject of sin. I might move through the lesson with the following questions: "How do most people deal with sin in their lives?" (A general type question.) "How can our group identify what are the right and wrong responses to sin?" (A community-oriented question.) "What are you going to do about it?" (A personal question.) At each stage the questions become more focused but the students have early opportunities to discuss the issue before taking on more challenging (and threatening) questions for their own lives.

3. The next tool helps us answer the question "How does God surprise me?" We need to know formational Bible study in order to understand and live God's Story ourselves. Formation is when we allow ourselves to become shaped and molded by the biblical story. This is not a blind behaviorism (being manipulated to act a certain

> **When we do learn to teach narratively, lives will change.**

way) but our intentional attempt to have our entire lives shaped into Christian character so that we are always open to hear what God has to say through Scripture. This is often a tough task since most of our reading is more focused on reading for information we can use rather than reading for formation so that God can use us! We need a way to read so that the Bible is less like a newspaper and more like a love letter from God. One way is to turn scripture into prayer through a devotional practice known as the *Lectio Divina* (divine reading). The steps are pretty simple.

(1) We first clear our busy minds, relax, and prepare to hear God in the scripture.

(2) We take time to read the passage slowly (perhaps several times) until we really "hear" the story.

(3) Next we let the Bible "speak" by becoming aware of the small portions of the passage (a verse, an image, an idea) that are important for us.

(4) We then pray to God about those issues, letting the Bible become the framework to direct our prayer toward God.

(5) We pause and wait quietly to see if God has anything else to say to us!

(6) We then close the time by thanking God both for the scripture and the opportunity to pray.

When we use this approach we learn that our lesson preparation and our devotional life become much richer. We are better teachers since we allow the Scripture to make a difference in our lives the same way we want it to make a difference in our students' lives. Ultimately we can use this approach not only to enhance our teaching but also to guide our students into a deeper appreciation of the Bible. We can teach and/or model this approach for our students so that they can learn to participate in their own formation into the very Christian character that we seek for all disciples.

4. Beyond teaching the story we need to *develop strategies for celebrating and living out God's Story.* Student responses can include community activities and personal application. We can arrange or plan service projects for our class, develop accountability groups to follow up on personal commitments and

explore ways to celebrate God's good news! Since some of these activities take time to plan, you may have to spend time well in advance of the lesson thinking of different ways for students to demonstrate their faith. Enlisting the help of other concerned adults may be crucial. Try to create a proposed activity list at least once a quarter and save any ideas you do not use. They may come in handy later.

5. Try to *connect the class to the larger church* (in discipleship and in ministry) so that they live beyond a week at a time. Our teaching is infinitely more effective if our lessons connect with the whole church throughout the week and across the year. One simple way to do this is to arrange your class to follow themes from the Christian calendar. The Christian calendar includes several of the key celebrations of the Church: Advent, Christmas, Epiphany, Lent, Easter, and Pentecost. You may want to discuss with your pastor how they can be used in your congregation. When you put the different seasons together they actually guide us through the birth, ministry, struggle, death, and resurrection of Jesus as well as the coming of the Holy Spirit and the birth of the Church. The more your lessons tie in to the broader activities of the congregation (including preaching and special events) the more your students will see the connection between what they study and how the Christian life is lived.

6. Finally we ask: "How do I know I have done my job?" Frankly, there are a lot of perils in evaluating our teaching. Teaching so that students change takes time, and we may not always see the fruit of our efforts. It does not hurt, however, to ask someone to evaluate our teaching on occasion to see if we are in a rut. This is best done when we have a team teacher or an assistant that we sometimes ask to pay attention to our teaching (rather than student reactions). Students can contribute as well. I often ask students what they would celebrate, change, or reconsider (three words that sound a lot better than evaluate) about the way a class is going. Rather than just focusing on student opinion, we want to look for real change in our students. What we are looking for are examples of story teaching becoming story living.

These tools can help each of us become better teachers. Like any other craft, it may take time to master them all. In time our teaching will be greatly enhanced by all of these activities.

We can learn to teach in such a way that we respect the power of story; we model our teaching on elements of the story; we follow the six steps; and we use the various tools to deepen our teaching. It may take some time to become comfortable and proficient in these steps. Remember that our goal is to be faithful in what we do, not absolutely master everything. When we do learn to teach narratively, lives will change (including our own!) and our students will become better Christians. What more can we ask?

CHAPTER 6

TEACHING

WITH

STYLE

JANELLE BEILER

Everyone loves stories. The film industry invests billions of dollars in producing stories because they know that people love to watch a good story. The publishing industry invests billions of dollars in telling stories in print because they know that people long to curl up with a good story. Television allows us to click through stories of various kinds—short stories, long and involved stories, stories that are stretched out in weekly episodes that pick up where the last one left off. Talk shows allow us to become familiar with celebrities and their stories. Talk shows also allow us the unique opportunity to enter into the stories of people and their problems. Even commercials are 30-second stories. Life is a story. That is why narrative teaching is so effective. Narrative teaching is based on the principle that the nature of what we are teaching is a story. The history of the world, the Bible, and the gospel are about an ongoing story, with God as the main character. The whole point of teaching is to tell *the* Story (God's Story) and show students how it affects *their* stories. This chapter will explore the many ways you can tell God's Story and invite your students to become part of that Story.

Learning Styles

To begin with, you must recognize that every student you teach is a unique, incredible, eternal person who was created by God. And when God created each of your students, He created him or her with a unique personality, preferences, and abilities. This uniqueness extends to the way students learn and organize information. The way a person learns best is called a learning style, which is often ingrained in a person from the time he or she is born into this world of sights, sounds, and sensations.

Babies have natural preferences for the way they prefer to be stimulated—through the ears, eyes, or skin. Listeners like sounds and words and often speak early, have large vocabularies, and learn to read easily. Lookers enjoy colors and shapes and motion. They often have above average eye-hand coordination and enjoy math. Movers crawl and stand ahead of schedule. They are confident with their bodies and are well coordinated. These natural tendencies may change over time, but people will eventually settle on their own preferred learning style. Of course, everyone uses all of his or her senses and therefore learns through various styles; still, we tend to prefer one or two dominant styles.

Therefore, in choosing the way you will teach a lesson and the methods you will use to tell God's Story, you will need to employ a variety of techniques so that you take into account the various learning styles your students have. To choose the appropriate methods suited to your students' learning styles, you will first need to identify what learning styles they have.

Over the years, many people have studied the way people learn and have come up with several different models of learning styles.[1] These models differ slightly depending on the part of learning they are analyzing. For example, Anthony D. Gregorc looked at perception (the way people take in information) and ordering (the way people organize and use the information they take in). He found a couple of different ways we perceive and a couple of ways we organize information. The combination of these four factors identifies our learning style.

Another researcher, Howard Gardner, observed people's strengths and abilities and determined that everyone is intelligent in certain areas. His model of learning styles, called multiple intelligences, identifies seven different ways people demonstrate intellectual ability.

One of the more widely used models is called the modality model, developed by Walter Barbe and Raymond Swassing. They identified three main sensory channels, or modes, through which we prefer to receive and remember information. These modes correspond to three of our basic senses—hearing, sight, and touch. Because of its simplicity and because it is easy to apply to a variety of learning situations, we will look at this model in a little more detail.

Auditory learners learn through their sense of hearing, by listening to and talking with others. They prefer to listen to someone read a book rather than to read it themselves. Auditory learners like to receive instructions verbally and they solve problems by talking through them aloud, especially in group settings. They remember information by speaking it aloud or repeating it over and over, often using rhythmic or musical patterns. Think about the students you teach and take a moment to identify one or two auditory learners. They are the ones who read aloud to themselves. They are probably the ones that you need to remind to be quiet. Here are some teaching methods that will likely appeal to auditory learners:

Agree-Disagree Discussion: Throw out a purposefully controversial statement related to your lesson and let the students take sides. Examples of hot topics are: abortion, suicide, cheating, the death penalty, politics, and so forth.

Brainstorming: Allow class members to suggest as many ideas as possible on a subject in a certain amount of time. Assign a recorder and be sure to enforce the "no idea is a dumb idea" rule. To make it a game, divide your students into groups and assign points for every idea.

Buzz Groups: Break a larger group into several small groups and give them a short amount of time to discuss a given topic. For fun, give each group a cassette recorder to record their conversation and then allow each group to play back their tape for the class.

Can of Worms: Place in a container questions or statements on issues written on separate slips of paper. Consider filling a can with gummy worms. Students can snack while they discuss and enjoy the gooey nature of the can as they reach in to select a paper.

Commercial Jingle: Instruct groups to write new words to the tunes of contemporary jingles to present a message from the session's scripture.

Debate: Select speakers to present opposing views on a controversial subject while the audience observes.

Interview: Appoint an on-the-spot reporter to present an imaginary interview with biblical/historical characters. Supply a microphone for a prop and assign a cameraman to make the role play livelier.

Neighbor Nudge: Assign class members into pairs to discuss a given question or subject for a short period of time.

Panel: Bring in several qualified persons to discuss given topics while your students observe and listen.

Word Association: Ask students to share the first thoughts that come to mind at the mention of a key word. To spice it up, set a short amount of time and have a loud timer ticking down to a loud buzz. (Games like Taboo and Guestures have good timers and buzzers.)

News Story/Headlines: Allow students to summarize Bible events in headlines or report about them in an imaginary news story. To make it easier, take a real newspaper and give permanent markers for students to adapt the already printed page.

Open-ended Story: Give small groups unfinished stories and ask them to complete them. One option is to provide an introduction and then go around the circle, allowing each student to add four words to the story.

Poetry: Ask students to respond to scriptural truth by composing their own poetry. Then provide a coffeehouse-type atmosphere to allow for a poetry reading. Rhyming and nonrhyming poetry may be used.

Lecture/Monologue/Sermon: Bring in a qualified individual to deliver a prepared verbal presentation.

Memory: Help students memorize selected scripture passages or other related material. Be sure to give them a chance to show off their hard work in front of a larger group.

Oral Reports: Give individual students the opportunity to share the results of their research, from individual or group work, with the class.

Recordings: Play a prerecorded song, lecture, or dialogue and allow your students to respond.

Visual learners learn through their sense of sight, by seeing and watching. They understand tasks and concepts best when illustrated with pictures or written descriptions. Visual learners remember best by recalling visual images and associations, such as a mental picture of the person who originally conveyed the information. Think about the students you teach and take a moment to identify the visual learners. They are the ones who may seem to be daydreaming when in reality they are visualizing in their minds what you are saying. Here are some methods that may appeal to visual learners:

Brochure: Provide materials for students to work in small groups to design a colorful folder promoting a session concept.

Banners: Display a key thought or verse from the session by designing and making a banner. Be sure to hang it up in your classroom or in a hallway when you are done.

Bulletin Board: A classroom bulletin board could be divided between small groups who decorate their section to correspond with the session theme.

Bumper Sticker: Create succinct scriptural reminders by writing on strips of paper in bumper sticker fashion. Use contact paper and students will actually be able to stick their bumper stickers to their cars or lockers.

Comic Strip: Allow students to illustrate a biblical story or contemporary application of Bible truth by creating several frames of cartoons.

Charts: Use charts to graphically display points of information on poster paper.

Coat of Arms: Instruct students to illustrate specific aspects of their life or the life of a Bible character by drawing three of four sections on a shield as a coat of arms.

Collage: Create an artistic composition made of various materials such as paper, wood, or cloth glued on a picture surface.

Frieze: Students can make a series of drawings or pictures that tell a chronological or continuing story.

Group Drawing: Have class members participate in making a drawing together that expresses a group opinion or discovery. This activity can be drawn out over several weeks of lessons, with students adding to the picture each week.

Graph: As small groups read a section of historical narrative, instruct them to graph the ups and downs of the Bible characters.

Instant Photos: Supply small groups with Polaroid cameras and instructions to locate and bring back a picture of a symbol of the lesson topic.

Tear It Up: Provide students with magazines, but no scissors. Have them tear words and/or pictures from the magazines to represent personal feelings or opinions.

Montage: Create a composite picture by combining several separate pictures. This activity can be used to represent different characters' points of view in a story.

Mural: Assign groups to work together to create a large painting or drawing on paper depicting a biblical event or practical application of scripture.

Painting: Watercolors or poster paints are effective media for individuals who wish to paint a realistic or impressionistic scriptural truth.

Slide Show: Assign groups to create original slides to be presented with live or recorded music or narration. This is a more long-term activity to spread over several weeks. Electronic slide shows using software such as Microsoft PowerPoint are popular and fairly easy to do.

Symbolic Shapes: Ask students to cut or tear shapes from color paper to symbolize a lesson idea.

Time Line: Ask class members to work together to visualize biblical event chronologically on work sheets or a length of butcher paper on the wall.

Visual Aids: Consider the use of the following visual aid instruments to include the sense of sight in the teaching/learning process: chalkboard, flip chart, overhead projector, videotape, filmstrips, charts, maps, diagrams, work sheets, demonstrations, and so forth.

Kinesthetic/tactile learners learn through the sense of touch, by touching, moving, or some other physical interaction. They may have difficulty sitting still for more than a few minutes at a time because they need to physically participate in a task. When they read or watch visual images, they prefer stories that are full of action. Tactile/kinesthetic learners remember best by repeating the same or by doing something with what has been learned. Think about the students you teach and take a moment to identify the tactile/kinesthetic learners. They are the ones who seem to fidget and move constantly. They can appear to be disrespectful when In reality they are doing their best to learn. Below are some methods for connecting with tactile and kinesthetic learners:

Videos: Give your students an opportunity to make their own videos out of class to illustrate a session truth. Then be sure to present their work in class or for the congregation.

Pantomime: Instruct students to act out a situation or portion of scripture without speaking.

Psychodrama: Allow students to act out their own life situations in order to gain insight into their feelings and behavior patterns. Then help them apply the lesson truth to their situation.

Case Study/Role Play: Give students specific problem situations to act out extemporaneously. Use real-life situations (case studies) drawn from newspapers, magazines, or other sources, or make up your own hypothetical situations (role play).

Skit: Have students plan and act out a situation that relates to the session.

Demonstration: Allow your students the opportunity to demonstrate specific tasks or skills related to the lesson. Then allow observers to practice what they have seen.

Display/Exhibit: Give students certain objects or materials to examine. If you are teaching about the woman caught in adultery, have a collection of large rocks for your students to hold to help them imagine the crowd standing around the woman, ready to stone her.

Field Trip: Travel outside the classroom to a location that is of interest and related to your lesson. To give students a feel for Jesus' teaching by the Sea of Galilee, travel to a large pond or seashore and teach the students.

Simulation Games: Let students reproduce real-life situations in a game format so that learners can simulate others' feelings, responses, and so forth.

This brief overview of the three main modes of learning should provide some insight into frustrations your students might feel if you frequently ignore their learning style. An auditory learner is going to be frustrated and unable to retain information when you use flash cards to memorize a Bible verse (especially if you enforce strict silence in the process!). A visual learner is going to be frustrated by frequent lectures and rare uses of visual aids, such as a bright poster or video clip.

It is important to know not only how your students learn best but also what *your* learning preference is. Most teachers tend to utilize the same type of methods when they teach that they learn best from. If you are an auditory learner, you will probably tend to be an auditory teacher and catch yourself saying, "Listen to me." If you are a visual learner, you are probably a visual teacher and you might catch yourself saying, "Look at me." If you are a tactile learner, you are probably a tactile teacher and might find that you tend to move while you teach and need to touch students on the arm, the head, the shoulder, in order to feel as though you have connected with them. When we know our learning style, we can be more conscious to use a variety of teaching methods that cater to the three learning styles of our students. Appendix D contains an interactive learning styles test. Fill out this test to determine your own learning style.

Find ways to use a variety of these teaching methods in each lesson and you will have students learning in ways that make them feel comfortable and confident. Remember, you are trying to tell a story with each lesson. You are telling a story for the purpose of bringing about change in the lives of your learners. You may have noticed that storytelling did not appear as a specific method in the lists above. We will now address storytelling as an overarching method that can incorporate other types of methods.

Maybe the thought of telling a story scares you. Some people are natural storytellers. They've got the voice for it, and for some reason, interesting, crazy things seem to happen to them and they have oodles of stories to tell. If you do have a master storyteller in your church or community, by all means, bring that person in for a session where a long, suspenseful story is the crux of the lesson. However, realize that you don't need to be a natural storyteller in order to use storytelling methods.

One way to learn how to use storytelling is to simply share your own story. In fact, it is important for your students to feel that they know about you and your life. Of course, this must be done appropriately. There are parts of your life that your students don't need to know. But they can learn from your life and you will be more real to them if you are open about your own journey.

Another way to tell a story is to use other teaching methods that appeal to the variety of learning styles your students have. Consider the story of Jesus calming the storm in Luke 8:22-25. While an auditory learner might benefit from hearing the account of that story straight from Scripture, a visual learner would appreciate a more detailed account and time to imagine the rocking of the boat, the spray of the ocean, the smell of the storm, the sound of the lightning. In fact, why not get fans set up around the room to become fierce winds? They can start out softly as a breeze and get turned up as you get into the heart of the storm. Hand out spray bottles filled with water for kids to spray as the rain comes down harder and harder. Try passing out flashlights and turn the lights out—you've got lightning! Why not shake a piece of sheet metal to create thunder? Getting students involved in the story will help them learn, and at the same time, you've created visual elements for your visual learners, sounds for your auditory learners, and lots of action and movement for your tactile learners.

Seeing or drawing a map of the Sea of Galilee where the story takes place would add another visual method. Letting kids share their boat sto-

Getting students involved in the story will help them learn.

ries from various fishing trips or excursions they've been on would add to the lesson as well. Going to a beach to tell the story would be a great possibility for those who live near an ocean or large lake.

Some methods for telling the story include reenactment and role play. By getting students physically involved in the telling of the story, they find themselves involved in the story itself! Doing a case study on a particular character also encourages students to find out about that person's story and how it affects their own story.

Learning Environments

Ironically, disturbances in the classroom are often a result of "The Clash of the Storytellers." As a teacher, you have the floor and desire to have everyone's attention. Meanwhile, Hannah and Jessica are sitting off to your right, doing some storytelling of their own! Managing the learning environment involves discipline, and the best discipline is preventative discipline. Just like children, your students need to know the boundaries. They need to know what is expected of them, and they need to know what will happen if boundaries are crossed. Set these up clearly and positively. When the boundaries are crossed, enforce the consequences firmly but kindly. Help them realize that they choose the way things will go, and don't be afraid to express your dismay or concern when they choose poorly: "Dan, I'm sorry that you have chosen to speak that way to Evan. You know that we are kind to each other here. I need to ask you apologize and choose another seat."

Realize that your expectations have a great deal to do with how your class will function. If you are expecting a group of teenagers to sit quietly with their hands folded, you will be miserably disappointed. As you learned in the chapter on development, teens are very much involved in getting a feel for how they can interact with their world; that's their job! And it isn't a quiet process. Does that mean that you should sit back and allow your room to be chaos? Absolutely not! But heading into your class time with realistic but clear expectations will free you to teach.

Your students are also affected by their surroundings. Take a moment to think about the room in which you teach. Is it comfortable? Is it too comfortable? For teenagers, a table and folding chairs is a bit cold and unfeeling, but beanbag chairs scattered all over the floor are probably too comfortable and possibly inappropriate. Is the ceiling sagging? Are the walls an ugly green color? Do the chairs squeak? Do the lights flicker? These details all contribute to the atmosphere of your room and therefore the atmosphere of your teaching.

Another environmental issue is the atmosphere. It might be interesting to find out how your students study best at home. How and when do they do their homework? Do they sit at the kitchen table or sprawl on the floor? Do they work in silence or do they need a television or radio on? Do they like bright lights or dim lights? Do they sit still or roam around the house?

Obviously, you cannot hope to meet every student's preference for a learning environment at the same time. However, you can find out what the majority needs and seek to provide that. It will also do wonders to have insight as to why others might have difficulty concentrating at times.

What about the emotional environment? Do your students look forward to coming to your class? Do they look forward to it because they know they will have fun, learn, and be nurtured and loved unconditionally? Or do they dread it because they know they will be made fun of and they feel like anything they say will be laughed at? It's very important to have a safe emotional environment for teaching, especially for insecure teenagers. They need to know that they belong, that they are free and safe to struggle and voice opinions that might not be popular. Be very intentional about creating a safe emotional environment. You may have to reprimand students by saying, "We don't speak to each other like that here." Set high expectations for the way your students should treat each other and you will be surprised at what develops over time.

To find the best way to teach your students, you have to become a student of your students. Notice when Jeremy gains confidence from reading aloud. Take note when a drama brings out the personality in the new shy girl. Learn who should and should not be paired up together for projects. Knowing your students and knowing their learning styles will go a long way in deciding which teaching techniques and methods to use. Remember, avoid having an entire lesson include only visually oriented teaching methods, or auditory ones. Do your best to mix and match so that everyone's style is addressed in some way.

Becoming familiar with the unique learning styles of your students and the teaching methods that they require is one way to celebrate the God-given uniqueness of your students. As a teacher, you can help them benefit from their strengths and learn to use them well. You can also encourage them in the areas of their weaknesses by acknowledging their limitations in a positive way. Be proud of the one who contributed in class even though it was tough for him or her. Let him or her know how proud you are!

The next time you walk into your room full of students—some looking bored, some bouncing off the walls—realize what amazing creations they are and celebrate the opportunity to be a part of their lives and to be a part of their story. What a great way to think of your calling as a teacher. When you teach, you are nurturing others along the way in their journey. You are helping to move them toward becoming fully who they were created to be. If there is something worth devoting yourself to, this is it! When God calls us, He calls us to give our best. As a teacher, make it your goal to teach well, to teach with style.

Conclusion

JIM HAMPTON

His name was Gary and he wasn't your typical youth worker. Gary was on disability because he had severe hemophilia. As a result, Gary wasn't able to participate in sports or other activities in which he might get hurt and possibly bleed to death.

Gary didn't play the guitar nor did he sing. But the one thing that Gary could do was invest himself in the lives of teenagers. Gary was always interested in what we were doing. Even though he could not participate in many of the activities that we participated in, that never stopped him from coming and watching. We could always count on looking at the audience and see Gary sitting there, cheering madly when we were introduced.

The one aspect that Gary brought to his role as a youth worker was his incredible ability to listen. He could sit and listen for hours as teens poured out their hearts to him. I remember many nights when he would have a bunch of guys over for a sleepover. We would stay up late playing games like Risk and Monopoly and eating snack food until we were about to pop. But mostly we would talk—about school, our parents, and most importantly, our relationship with Jesus.

But Gary did more than just listen. He practiced the ideas that have been outlined in this book. He understood teenagers. He knew how we thought and acted, and he used this information to help him better know how to respond to us.

Gary also understood the inherent nature of adopting a narrative methodology. Now don't misunderstand me. Gary was not a trained theologian, and he would not have been able to give a succinct overview of the narrative methodology outlined in chapter 5. But Gary intrinsically knew how to teach. He knew that we needed more than just a couple of good words each week. He realized that we needed life transformation. And so he endeavored to make the lessons come alive by inviting us into a story that was so much bigger than we could imagine. He shared the stories of the heroes of the faith, detailing both their victories and their struggles. Gary wasn't content to just tell us the biblical stories. He also ed from his own life, showing us his victories and struggles, helping us see the contemporary possibilities of the Story of God for our own lives.

Perhaps most importantly, Gary understood the need to serve as a guide for his students. He seemed to always know what we were dealing with, and most important, how to help us discover and put into practice the Christian response to the problem. He was willing to walk alongside us, answering our questions and helping us think through the tough issues. He seemed to know when to push us and when we needed some space. And Gary did all of this because he realized that his primary job was to help his students develop a lifelong identity of being Christian.

The fact that you have read this book tells me that you are a lot like Gary. You love your students and you want to help them find their place in the Story of God. You want to help them develop an identity that is based in Christ and not the things of this world. You earnestly desire that they develop a lifelong faith in Christ and are willing to give of yourself, walking alongside them, to help make this happen.

You have before you a most incredible opportunity: the opportunity to help students find their place in the Story of God as you walk with them as guides. We understand that being a guide for students is not an easy job, nor is it always appreciated. In fact, it is sometimes easy to wonder whether we are making any impact at all. Teaching is hard work with seemingly few rewards. But please know that your church appreciates it, the parents of the youth you teach appreciate it, and even though they may not say it very often, your students appreciate your investment in them. And please know that the authors of this book have the highest respect for what you are doing as you help shape and form young people. When we invest our lives in our students, we can never know just how God can use us.

We believe that there is no higher calling one can have than to lead students to find their place in the Story of God. You have chosen to obey that call, and for that you are to be commended.

As we close this book, let us offer this blessing:
May Jesus Christ, the Master Teacher, guide and strengthen you as you work to help youth find their place in His Story. May you be emboldened as you seek to become *Theotokos*, Godbearers, to your students. And may God's grace envelop you as you follow Him. Amen.

Appendix A

Living Life by the Christian Calendar

STEPHEN GREEN

How should we use or "order" our time? One of the top priorities for our churches is to help people organize their lives within sacred time. I am convinced that the sanctifying of life occurs as secular time is transformed into sacred time. A tool to encourage this to happen for us is the use of the Church's calendar.

Over many centuries, the Christian Church year evolved with seasons and days of recognition. In time, different Christian communities have adapted or adopted, and simplified or expanded, the Christian calendar. Most churches still recognize six seasons and a variety of special days.

The Christian Calendar

The Christian year begins at Advent, the four-week season that precedes Christmas. Readings that speak of hope and expectation are used in worship. An Advent wreath is commonly used. Each week the appropriate number of candles are lit in order to designate how close Christmas has come.

Following Advent is the 12-day season of Christmas, during which we celebrate the Nativity of our Lord. Christmas extends from December 25 until January 6. It is a time of joy for promises kept and hopes fulfilled.

The season of Epiphany begins on January 6 and runs until the beginning of Lent at Ash Wednesday. The day of Easter, fixed by a lunar formula, determines when Ash Wednesday appears in the calendar. Thus, Epiphany varies in length from year to year but its meaning remains the same—the unfolding to the world of the nature and power of the Christ just born. It is a time of reflection on commitment to Jesus as the One offered to fulfill human needs and longings.

Lent begins on Ash Wednesday and lasts for 40 days, excluding Sundays, until Easter day. The season begins with the encroachment of ashes, a practice reclaimed from the historic church by many in contemporary worship. Lent is marked by additional times of devotion and personal reflection. It is a season to come to terms with ourselves, on the heels of being asked to come to terms with Jesus. It is a time to recognize our responsibility in the shortcomings of the world that can deny the one who is acknowledged as Lord. Lent turns the tables on us.

Holy Week concludes Lent and is marked by the use of palm branches. Maundy Thursday Communion recalls the Last Supper and the offering of the great commandment. Good Friday features a vigil of penitence.

The season of Easter begins with the celebration of the resurrection of Jesus. The theme is always the theme of new life and renewal. The celebration of Holy Communion at Easter commonly takes place as an experience shared with those first disciples for whom the risen Christ was made known in the breaking of the bread and the pouring of the wine. The season lasts for 50 days until the Day of Pentecost. The entire season is one of joy and belief in the possibilities of overcoming the barriers imposed by the powers of destruction in our world.

The Day of Pentecost is a celebration of the birth of the church and the coming of the Holy Spirit to our community. It begins the half-year of the church. We call the days of Pentecost "ordinary days"—routine days during which we experience growth and development. These are days of nurturing in the church, the family of God's people.

The power and presence of the Holy Spirit becomes the source of faith, comfort, and strength to move forward and engage the world around us in efforts to advance the realm of God. This is a long season as befits a time of pilgrimage and nurturing.

A Mirror of Human Experience

Practice of the Christian year is spiritually powerful because its themes mirror our human experience so completely that we are able to link ourselves with Jesus Christ and the community of faith in ways that endure. As normal human beings, we live our lives with the same dynamics that the Christian year acknowledged. We approach life with hope and expectation (Advent). It is hope that allows us to set goals, plan, and move forward. It is hope that enables us to envision new days and make things happen for the good. Life without expectation—Advent—is an empty life.

Personal strength is built upon hopes being realized and promises fulfilled—Christmas. To know that promises can be kept is the basis for trust in all our lives. Christmas assures us that we can live with trust, even in our world.

Human life is also marked by the process of unfolding wisdom. Epiphany mirrors this human dynamic and helps us make truth our own and formulate our beliefs.

As human beings we also need to come to terms with our shortcomings. We need to see the part that we contribute to the barriers that exist in human relationships in our world. We need to come to terms with failure. Lent is our time of being honest with ourselves—the spiritual parallel to the watershed experience in human life.

To be alive is to find new direction and resolve in the aftermath of falling short. To live full lives we need to go forward. Trouble cannot be the final word in our human experience. Easter is the spiritual word for the human experience of new beginnings and opportunities.

Most of life is spent in routine. We do what we have to do. We develop relationships and find moments of peace and joy. Pentecost is the spiritual parallel of this process—the time of growth and maturity in the routine of life.

The ordering of time within the Christian year is the portrayal of living a full human existence. It combines the realities of human living with the message of Holy Scripture—it is daring to live within the Story of God! As you look upon your calendar, daytimer, and watch, be ever mindful of the arrangement of time . . . may it be sacred time!

Appendix B
Themes of the Christian Calendar

Advent—Four Sundays preceding Christmas Day
Themes:
- The light of Christ coming into the world's darkness
- The messengers of God bringing good news to the hurting
- Believers preparing for Christmas worship and celebration
- Believers preparing for the Second Coming (Second Advent)
- Believers recognizing the darkness around them but living in light

Christmas—Christmas Day through 12 days ending on January 6 (Epiphany)
Themes:
- The birth of Christ
- God with us—"Immanuel"
- God understands us, knows us, loves us, wants to be near us
- Believers celebrating more than nostalgia, sentimentality, hedonism

Epiphany—January 6 ending on Transfiguration Sunday (the Sunday before Ash Wednesday)
Themes:
- God making himself known to the world
- Salvation coming to the world
- Christ made known to the magi
- Christ made known at the baptism
- Christ beginning His earthly ministry
- Christ made known through parables, teachings, and miracles
- The transfiguration of Christ
- Believers discerning God's will and purpose for their lives
- Believers following God's leading
- Believers living counterculturally in the kingdom of God
- Also called the "Season of Light," continuing the Advent/Christmas theme

Lent—Ash Wednesday (40 days, not counting Sundays, before Easter Sunday) through Holy Saturday (the day before Easter)

Themes:
- Christ tempted in the wilderness for 40 days
- Christ in the last days of His earthly ministry
- Believers confessing their fragility and dependence (Ash Wednesday)
- Believers pursuing the life of discipleship
- Believers examining their lives for evidence of sin and righteousness
- Believers preparing for Easter celebration and worship
- Believers deepening their spiritual life and drawing near to Christ
- Historically, a time of baptismal instruction and preparation

Easter—Easter Sunday through Pentecost Sunday

Themes:
- The resurrection of Christ
- The victory of Christ over sin and death
- The post-Resurrection appearances of Christ
- The ascension of Christ
- The healing of brokenness, the forgiveness of sins, the strength to live victoriously

Pentecost—the Sunday seven weeks after Easter

Themes:
- The coming of the Holy Spirit
- The creation of the Church
- The gifting of the Church into the world
- The unity and diversity of the Church
- Whole-life stewardship

Ordinary Time—the time between Pentecost Sunday and the first Sunday of Advent

Appendix C
Measuring Faith Maturity

Read each statement in this self-test and decide how well it fits you. Write the appropriate number next to the statement. Choose your responses from these options:

1 = never true
2 = rarely true
3 = true once in a while
4 = sometimes true
5 = often true
6 = almost always true
7 = always true

_____ 1. Every day I see evidence that God is active in the world.

_____ 2. I feel a deep sense of responsibility for reducing pain and suffering in the world.

_____ 3. I am spiritually moved by the beauty of God's creation.

_____ 4. I care a great deal about reducing poverty in my country and throughout the world.

_____ 5. I devote time to reading and studying the Bible.

_____ 6. I do things to help protect the environment.

_____ 7. I have a real sense that God is guiding me.

_____ 8. I am concerned that our country is not doing enough to help the poor.

_____ 9. I like to worship and pray with others.

_____ 10. I give significant portions of time and money to help other people.

_____ 11. I seek out opportunities to help me grow spiritually.

_____ 12. I go out of my way to show love to people I meet.

_____ 13. I take time for periods of prayer or meditation.

_____ 14. I speak out for equality among all people.

_____ 15. I talk with other people about my faith.

_____ 16. I think Christians must be about the business of creating inter-national understanding and harmony.

_____ 17. My faith helps me to know right from wrong.

_____ 18. I try to apply my faith to political and social issues.

_____ 19. My faith shapes the way I think and act each and every day.

_____ 20. In my free time, I help people who have problems or needs.

_____ 21. My life is filled with meaning and purpose.

_____ 22. I am active in efforts to promote world peace.

_____ 23. As I grow older, my understanding of God changes.

_____ 24. I am active in efforts to promote world peace.

To identify your "faith type" follow this process:

First, add together the sum of the fives, sixes, and sevens you wrote in the *odd*-numbered statements. The result is your *vertical* score.

Next, add together the sum of the fives, sixes, and sevens you wrote in the *even*-numbered statements. The result is your *horizontal* score.

Finally, discover your "faith type," using the following key:

If both your horizontal and vertical scores are higher than 60, you have a *mature* or *integrated faith*. A Christian with an integrated faith experiences both a life-transforming relationship with God and a devotion to serving others.

If your horizontal score is greater than 60 but your vertical score is less than 60, you have a *horizontal faith*. A Christian with a horizontal faith is devoted to serving others but lacks a life-transforming relationship with God.

If your vertical score is greater than 60 but your horizontal score is less than 60, you have a *vertical faith*. A Christian with a vertical faith has a life-transforming relationship with God but lacks a devotion to serving others.

If both your horizontal and vertical scores are below 60, you have an *undeveloped faith*. Christians with undeveloped faith do not strongly exhibit their faith through either serving others or a life-transforming relationship with God.

Adapted from Eugene C. Roehlkepartain, *The Teaching Church* (Nashville: Abingdon Press, 1993). Used by permission.

Appendix D

Interactive Learning Styles Test

Everybody has a preferred learning style. Knowing and understanding our learning style helps us learn more effectively. Through identifying your learning style, you will be able to capitalize on your strengths and improve your teaching skills.

Directions: Place a check in all the boxes that describe you. The list with the greatest number of checks is your dominant learning style.

List 1—Tactile/Kinesthetic Learning Style

- ☐ Reach out to touch things
- ☐ Collect things
- ☐ Talk fast, using hands to communicate what they want to say
- ☐ Constantly fidgeting (e.g., tapping pen, playing with keys in pocket)
- ☐ Good at sports
- ☐ Like to take things apart, put things together
- ☐ Prefer to stand while working
- ☐ Like to have music in the background while working
- ☐ Enjoy working with hands and making things
- ☐ Like to chew gum or eat in class
- ☐ Learn through movement and exploring the environment around them
- ☐ May be considered hyperactive
- ☐ Good at finding their way around
- ☐ Comfortable touching others as a show of friendship (e.g., hugging)
- ☐ Prefer to do things rather than watching a demonstration or reading about it in a book

List 2—Visual Learning Style

- ☐ Ask for verbal instructions to be repeated
- ☐ Watch speakers' facial expressions and body language
- ☐ Like to take notes to review later
- ☐ Remember best by writing things down several times or drawing pictures and diagrams
- ☐ Are good spellers
- ☐ Turn the radio or TV up really loud

- ☐ Get lost with verbal instructions
- ☐ Prefer information to be presented visually (e.g., flip charts or chalk board)
- ☐ Skillful at making graphs, charts, and other visual displays
- ☐ Can understand and follow directions on maps
- ☐ Feel the best way to remember something is to picture it in their head
- ☐ Follow written instructions better than oral ones.
- ☐ Good at solving jigsaw puzzles
- ☐ Get the words to a song wrong
- ☐ Good at the visual arts

List 3—Auditory Learning Style

- ☐ Follows verbal directions better than written ones
- ☐ Would rather listen to a lecture than read the material in a textbook
- ☐ Understand better when they read aloud
- ☐ Struggle to keep notebooks neat
- ☐ Prefer to listen to the radio rather than read a newspaper
- ☐ Frequently sing, hum or whistle to themselves
- ☐ Dislike reading from a computer screen especially when the backgrounds are fussy
- ☐ When presented with two similar sounds, can tell if sounds are the same or different
- ☐ Require explanations of diagrams, graphs, or maps
- ☐ Enjoy talking to others
- ☐ Talk to themselves
- ☐ Use musical jingles to learn things
- ☐ Would rather listen to music than view a piece of artwork
- ☐ Use finger as a pointer when reading
- ☐ Like to tell jokes and stories and makes verbal analogies to demonstrate a point

This learning styles test was adapted from Elizabeth Bogod (an adult with learning disabilities). Further information regarding learning styles may be found by visiting LD Pride Online—http://www.ldpride.net—an on-line community for youth and adults with learning disabilities, promoting the positive side of learning disabilities and attention deficit/hyperactivity disorder. Used with permission.

Notes

Chapter 1

1. "The leading edge of the Millennial generation were babies in the early 1980's" (William Howe and Neil Strauss, *The Fourth Turning* [New York: Broadway Books, 1997], 59). "Roughly, analysts start with Americans born in 1980, the first who will turn 21 in the next century" (Elizabeth Large, "A New Generation Won't Be Typecast but It's Taking Shape," *The Baltimore Sun,* May 1, 1999).

2. "About 95% of the nation's teens listen to FM radio, averaging more than 10 hours each week. . . . To teens, radio means music. . . . Radio programming is almost exclusively comprised, then, of what teens love best" (Peter Zollo, "Not Quite the TV Generation," *American Demographics,* May 1999).

3. "Nielsen Media Research has found that younger teens today watch less TV than the 18-49 age group, and spend more time online than any other demographic" (Cristina Merrill, "Keeping Up with Teens," *American Demographics,* October 1999, 30).

4. Thirty-three percent of U.S. teens are minorities (28 percent of all Americans are minorities) (David Foster, "Class of 2000 Facing Hopes, Fears," The Associated Press, September 11, 1999).

5. In 2001, 18 percent of babies born in U.S. will be Hispanic; by 2005, Hispanic youth will be the largest ethnic youth population in U.S. (Helene Stapinski, "Generación Latino," *American Demographics,* July 1999).

6. Fifty-three percent of teens said they have at least one close friend of another race or ethnic group. Ibid., 65.

7. Patricia Hersch, *A Tribe Apart* (New York: Fawcett, 1998). A wake-up call for all parents and teenagers, this essential book is also hopeful. Hersch urges us not to be afraid of teenagers—even if they have piercings and tattoos and strange hair—because what they really, truly want is a little guidance, attention, and love.

Chapter 3

1. The majority of faith dropouts occur during the high school years, rather than after graduation, as is commonly assumed.

2. Initial findings of yet to be published research by Roland Martinson.

Chapter 5

1. For a further look at narrative teaching, check out these resources by Thomas Groome: *Christian Religious Education: Sharing Our Story and Vision* (San Francisco: Harper and Row Publishers, 1980), 184-231, and *Sharing Faith: A Comprehensive Approach to Religious Education and Pastoral Ministry* (San Francisco: Harper and Row Publishers, 1991), 133-74.

2. The authors are indebted to Thomas Groome for his book *Christian Religious Education: Sharing Our Story and Vision,* which serves as one primary method that shapes narrative teaching.

3. Whether you use a direct question concerning each student's personal behavior or a more general description of other people's behavior depends on the amount of trust the students have in you as a teacher and with each other. This will be explained later in the chapter when we discuss asking the right questions.

Chapter 6

1. For more complete descriptions of the following learning styles models, plus others, see Cynthia Ulrich Tobias, *The Way They Learn* (Wheaton, Ill.: Tyndale House Publishers, 1994).

Recommended Resources

Youth Culture

Mueller, Walt. 1999. *Understanding Today's Youth Culture* (revised edition). Carol Stream, Ill.: Tyndale House Publishers.

Rainer, Thomas. 1997. *The Bridger Generation*. Nashville: Broadman and Holman Publishing.

Sweet, Leonard. 1999. *SoulTsunami: Sink or Swim in the New Millennium Culture*. Grand Rapids: Zondervan.

Narrative

Achtemeier, Elizabeth. 1989. *Preaching from the Old Testament*. Louisville: Westminster/John Knox Press.

Clapp, Rodney. 1996. *A Peculiar People: The Church as Culture in a Post-Christian Society*. Downers Grove, Ill.: InterVarsity Press.

Ellingsen, Mark. 1990. *The Integrity of Biblical Narrative: Story in Theology and Proclamation*. Minneapolis: Augsburg Fortress Press.

Hauerwas, Stanley, and William H. Willimon. 1989. *Resident Aliens: Life in the Christian Colony*. Nashville: Abingdon Press.

Lowry, Eugene. 1980. *The Homiletical Plot: The Sermon as Narrative Art Form*. Louisville: Westminster/John Knox Press.

Teaching

Anderson, Herbert, and Edward Foley. 1998. *Mighty Stories, Dangerous Rituals: Weaving Together the Human and the Divine*. San Francisco: Jossey-Bass Publishers.

Edie, Fred. 1998. *Sunday School CPR: How to Breathe New Life into Sunday Morning*. Nashville: Abingdon Press.

Groome, Thomas H. 1980. *Christian Religious Education: Sharing Our Story and Vision*. San Francisco: Jossey-Bass Publishers.

Hestenes, Roberta. 1985. *Using the Bible in Groups*. Louisville: Westminster/John Knox Press.

LeFever, Marlene. 1996. *Creative Teaching Methods*. Colorado Springs: D.C. Cook.

Palmer, Parker. 1998. *The Courage to Teach*. San Francisco: Jossey-Bass Publishers.

Robert, Richard. 1992. *Teaching for Faith: A Guide for Teachers of Adult Classes*. Louisville: Westminster/John Knox Press.

Vest, Norvene. 1997. *Gathered in the Word: Praying the Scripture in Small Groups*. Nashville: Upper Room Books.

Spiritual Formation

Dean, Kenda Creasy, and Ron Foster. 1998. *The Godbearing Life: The Art of Soul Tending for Youth Ministry.* Nashville: Upper Room Books.

Discipleship Journal. Christianity Today, Inc.

Foster, Richard. 1998. *Celebration of Discipline.* San Francisco: HarperCollins Publishers.

Mulholland, M. Robert, Jr. 1993. *Invitation to a Journey: A Road Map for Spiritual Formation.* Downers Grove, Ill.: InterVarsity Press.

Peterson, Eugene H. 1980. *A Long Obedience in the Same Direction: Discipleship in an Instant Society.* Downers Grove, Ill.: InterVarsity Press.

Stowell, Joseph M. 1998. *Far from Home.* Chicago: Moody Press.

Tracy, Wesley, et al. 1994. *The Upward Call.* Kansas City: Beacon Hill Press of Kansas City.

Willard, Dallas. 1988. *The Spirit of the Disciplines.* San Franciso: Harper San Francisco.

Learning Styles

Tobias, Cynthia Ulrich. 1996. *Every Child Can Succeed.* Colorado Springs: Focus on the Family Publishing.

———. 1994. *The Way They Learn.* Carol Stream, Ill.: Tyndale House Publishers.

Internet Resources

Center for Parent-Youth Understanding: http://www.cpyu.org

Challenge 2000: http://www.challenge2000.com

Entertainment Weekly: http://cgi.pathfinder.com/ew

Group: http://www.grouppublishing.com

International Lyrics Server: http://www.lyrics.ch.index.htm

Internet Movie Database: http://www.imdb.com

Princeton Religion Research Center: http://www.prrc.com

Search Institute: http://www.search-institute.org

Screen It! Entertainment Reviews for Parents: http://www.screenit.com

Youth Pastor.com: http://www.youthpastor.com

Youth Specialties: http://www.youthspecialties.com

Reference List

Buechner, Frederick. 1983. *Now and Then*. San Francisco: Harper and Row.

———. 1991. *Telling Secrets*. New York: HarperCollins.

Carnegie Council on Adolescent Development. *Great Transitions: Preparing Adolescents for a New Century*. New York: Carnegie Corporation of New York.

Clayton, Mark. "Colleges Turn to Peer Pressure to Curb Drinking." *The Christian Science Monitor*, October 27, 1997.

Cimino, Richard, and Don Lattin. "Choosing My Religion." *American Demographics*, April 1999.

Daloz, Laurent. 1987. *Effective Teaching and Mentoring*. San Francisco: Jossey-Bass.

Dean, Kenda Creasy, and Ron Foster. 1998. *The Godbearing Life: The Art of Soul Tending for Youth Ministry*. Nashville: Upper Room Books.

DeVries, Mark. 1994. *Family-Based Youth Ministry: Reaching the Been-There, Done-That Generation*. Downers Grove, Ill.: InterVarsity Press.

Foster, David. "Class of 2000 Facing Hopes, Fears." The Associated Press. September 11, 1999.

Franey, Lynn. "New Method Tried to Reduce Drinking Among College Students." *Kansas City Star*, November 28, 2000.

Hampton, Jim, and Rick Edwards. 1999. *Writer's Guidelines for WordAction Youth Curriculum*. Kansas City: Sunday School Ministries Division, The Church of the Nazarene.

Hersch, Patricia. 1998. *A Tribe Apart*. New York: Fawcett.

Howe, William, and Neil Strauss. 1997. *The Fourth Turning*. New York: Broadway Books.

Kipke, Michele, ed. 1999. *Adolescent Development and the Biology of Puberty: Summary of a Workshop on New Research*. Washington, D.C.: National Academy Press.

Large, Elizabeth. "A New Generation Won't Be Typecast but It's Taking Shape." *The Baltimore Sun*, March 1, 1999.

Merrill, Cristina. "Keeping Up with Teens." *American Demographics*, October 1999.

Nouwen, Henri. 1993. *In the Name of Jesus: Reflections on Christian Leadership*. New York: Crossroad.

Palmer, Parker. 1998. *The Courage to Teach: Exploring the Inner Landscape of a Teacher's Life*. San Francisco: Jossey-Bass.

Search Institute. 1990. *Effective Christian Education: A National Study of Protestant Congregations*. Minneapolis.

Stapinski, Helene. "Generación Latino." *American Demographics*, July 1999.

"Statistics on Class of 2000." The Associated Press, September 11, 1999.

Steele, Les. 1990. *On the Way: A Practical Theology of Christian Formation*. Grand Rapids: Baker Books.

"Teen Star." *Kansas City Star*, December 22, 2000.

Tobias, Cynthia Ulrich. 1994. *The Way They Learn*. Wheaton, Ill.: Tyndale House Publishers.

Vogel, Linda J. 1991. *Teaching and Learning in Communities of Faith*. San Francisco: Jossey-Bass.

Zollo, Peter. "Not Quite the TV Generation." *American Demographics,* May 1999.

Zustiak, Gary. 1996. *The Next Generation*. Joplin, Mo.: College Press Publishing.

Contributors

Jim Hampton is the executive editor for Nazarene Youth International Ministries, Church of the Nazarene, Kansas City.

Tim Green is chaplain and chair of the Department of Religion at Trevecca Nazarene University, Nashville.

Rick Edwards is the executive editor for WordAction Youth Sunday School Curriculum, Kansas City.

Mark Hayse is the associate pastor of education and youth at Shawnee Church of the Nazarene, Shawnee, Kansas.

Dean Blevins is associate professor of Christian education at Trevecca Nazarene University, Nashville.

Janelle Beiler is the children's pastor at Salisbury Church of the Nazarene, Salisbury, Maryland.